LATCRIT

LatCrit

From Critical Legal Theory to Academic Activism

Francisco Valdes and Steven W. Bender

*With a Foreword by Margaret E. Montoya and an
Afterword by Sumi Cho and Angela P. Harris*

NEW YORK UNIVERSITY PRESS
New York

NEW YORK UNIVERSITY PRESS
New York
www.nyupress.org

References to Internet websites (URLs) were accurate at the time of writing. Neither the author nor New York University Press is responsible for URLs that may have expired or changed since the manuscript was prepared.

Library of Congress Cataloging-in-Publication Data
Names: Valdes, Francisco, 1954– author. | Bender, Steven, author.
Title: LatCrit : from critical legal theory to academic activism / Francisco Valdes and Steven W. Bender ; with a foreword by Margaret E. Montoya and an afterword by Sumi Cho and Angela P. Harris. Other titles: Latina/o critical race theory
Description: New York : New York University Press, [2021] | Includes bibliographical references and index.

Identifiers: LCCN 2020050144 | ISBN 9781479809295 (hardback) | ISBN 9781479809301 (paperback) | ISBN 9781479809325 (ebook) | ISBN 9781479809318 (ebook other)

Subjects: LCSH: Discrimination in education—Law and legislation—United States. | Discrimination in higher education—Law and legislation—United States. | Racism in education—United States. | Race discrimination—Law and legislation—United States. | Critical pedagogy—United States.

Classification: LCC KF4155 .V349 2021 | DDC 340.071/173—dc23

LC record available at https://lccn.loc.gov/2020050144
New York University Press books are printed on acid-free paper, and their binding materials are chosen for strength and durability. We strive to use environmentally responsible suppliers and materials to the greatest extent possible in publishing our books.

Manufactured in the United States of America

10 9 8 7 6 5 4 3 2 1

Also available as an ebook

We dedicate this book to our beloved friend and colleague Jerome McCristal Culp, Jr. (1950–2004). Your kind but edgy life, work, and being exuded the values, integrity, and praxis to which we all aspire. You're still inspiring and guiding us forward, Jerome!

CONTENTS

FOREWORD

The Gran Trecho *That Is LatCrit*

MARGARET E. MONTOYA

> When "I" is replaced with "We," even illness becomes
> wellness.
> —Malcolm X

Timing can be a gift, and this is the right time for this book. The current
Black Lives Matter (BLM) movement's demands for justice are focused
primarily on Black people and their suffering through 400 years of cru-
elty and oppression coupled with passing attention to the genocide and
erasure of Indigenous and tribal people. A key aspect of the LatCrit project (short for Latina and Latino Critical Legal Theory), as described in
this timely book, is the centering and elaboration of Latinx identity in
law and policy without essentializing this variegated and multifaceted
identity that embraces race, color, ethnicity, language, sexual orientation,
gender identity, immigration status, national origin, and so on. To be
clear, the identifier "Latinx" personifies the Spanish settler-colonialism
that conquered much of this hemisphere and whose predations resulted
in the mestizo/mulatto populations of Spanish–African–Indian
ancestry—people whose physical appearance or phenotype varies significantly. According to Pew Research Center as of 2016, 24 percent of U.S.
Latinx identify as Afro-Latinx or Black Latinx,[1] and 34 percent identify
as "mestizo, mulatto or some other mixed race."[2] Some, especially Black
and Indigenous youth, challenge and interrogate the Latinx/Hispanic/

Latin American labels as erasures of race, U.S. imperialism, and Indigenous sovereignty;[3] others connect the Latinx label with the ruling classes of Mexico and Latin America; while a few choose Indigenous terms such as the Nahuatl *Mazewalli*, meaning an "Indigenous person."[4] We in LatCrit acknowledge the historical tensions (emerging from imperialism and *mestizaje*) between Latinx and Black or Indigenous communities, tensions that are evidenced by concerns named above as well as the liminality of mixed-raced identities, the historical amnesia about the extent of African slavery in the Americas, the overclaiming or denial of Indigenous ancestry, and the displacement of Black, Indigenous, and tribal people, often by more assimilated, lighter-skinned Latinxs. We also acknowledge such contemporary atrocities as the forgotten Indigenous women and girls, such as Anthonette Christine Cayedito, who are missing or murdered at rates that are 10 times the national average.[5] (These issues are particularly salient for those of us who live in close proximity to Indian Country or in areas with a smaller Black polity; New Mexico is home to twenty-three Indigenous pueblos, tribes, and nations but has fewer than 2 percent Black residents.) This type of analysis—the unpacking associated with identity, racial labels, color hierarchies, contested histories, and the meaning given to memory—has been an important dimension of interrogating who belongs in LatCrit as it has sought to deepen its critical commitments to democratic, Big Tent practices of inclusion, multidimensional discourse, and intentional programmatic diversity.

The work of this book is to describe the emergence of LatCrit principles, jurisprudence, community-building methods, praxis, pedagogy, and governance practices. Coming after Critical Legal Studies and Critical Race Theory (CRT) as academic formations, LatCrit had the benefit of previous successes and stumbles. LatCrit emphasized Latinx identities, lived experience, and policy concerns while rejecting Latinx exceptionalism and insistently maintaining an intersectional discourse and cultivating a diverse, participatory community. From its inception and as detailed in the extensive endnotes of this book, LatCrit has benefited from the contributions of scholars from many backgrounds; Black scholars such as Jerome McCristal Culp, Jr., and Angela Harris played an indispensable role in LatCrit's development; LatCrit would not be what it became without them and other key leaders such as Sumi Cho as well as Frank Valdes and Steve Bender (the coauthors of this book) and so many others too numerous to mention.

LatCrit has formally, through its programming, and informally, through its hospitality venues, engendered debates between and among scholars from the various racial groups, revealing over and over that racial depravity, oppression, and everyday humiliation are the manifestations of interwoven and cross-pollinating systems of oppression. LatCrit practices were designed to center and de-center different identities in a rotating process: these organizational processes were intended to produce knowledge and cultivate community that reflected many voices and views. Thus, the BLM agenda of centering Black (and Indigenous) communities is both a new challenge to all groups and individuals working for social justice (including LatCrit) as well as part of LatCrit's ongoing inquiries and programs.

The path that originally led me to LatCrit runs through the Critical Race Theory literature that I delved into during the writing of my first publication, "*Máscaras, Trenzas y Greñas*: The Un/Masking of the Self While Un/Braiding Latina Stories and Legal Discourse."[6] Even as an undergraduate, my racial consciousness was nurtured by the African and Black intelligentsia. I took Chicano Studies classes at San Diego State University in 1971–1972 in a department named "Mexican-American Studies." In the early years (1968–1975), the students ran the department, including hiring and firing faculty as well as teaching classes.[7] As a teaching assistant, I remember that our classes were inspired by, and we encouraged participation in, the burgeoning Chicano Movement. Our assigned readings drew from Marxism but also from the African liberation scholarship of Franz Fanon and Albert Memmi as well as the writings of Dr. Martin Luther King, Jr., and Malcolm X. Chicanas/os, as we called ourselves at the time, were just beginning to be admitted to graduate and professional schools through affirmative action programs; ethnic studies scholars and their books would appear after I left San Diego. Once I began my academic career, my thinking and writing were greatly influenced by the early CRT African American icons, such as Patricia Williams, Chuck Lawrence, and Kimberlé Crenshaw.

I have recounted in my writing and talks that, being hyper-aware of the underrepresentation and invisibility of Latinx people in the public square, I enter meetings looking for Brown faces, Spanish names, and other identity clues and cues. In LatCrit, I found a community that shared my Latinx worldview while expanding my understanding of and involvement with other Outsider communities and identities. But during this time of multiple crises, what does it mean to recalibrate our Latinx commitments centering anti-Black racism (and Indigenous marginality) and creating explicit conjunctions with LatCrit principles, methods, and motivations? How do we engage in the kind of self-critique—a LatCrit core value—to ensure that we are attentive to the cries in the streets for justice for Black people?

As I write this foreword, the United States is facing five existential crises at once, and all have stark racial implications of the type that make LatCrit theory and Critical Race Theory, its companion discourse, particularly relevant. The five crises are: (1) unrelenting police violence, as typified by the brazen police murders of George Floyd, Breonna Taylor, Tony McDade, Ahmaud Arbery, and many more, reinvigorating a massive BLM movement voicing a spectrum of injustice issues;[8] (2) an out-of-control COVID-19 pandemic; (3) an economy in Great Depression–level distress with unsustainable inequalities; (4) an incompetent, faltering federal government under a president (Donald Trump) whose reelection campaign is defined by white ethnonationalist messages; and (5) climate change—perhaps irremediable—menacing human life as we know it but for now pushed to the background. That five epic catastrophes could converge and concatenate at one time seems inconceivable. What has become clear is that the entanglement of these catastrophes requires a set of sophisticated racial tools to understand their disproportionate impacts on the multiply diverse communities of Black, Indigenous, and other People of Color (BIPOC).

Black Lives Matter

I was conversing with my younger daughter, Alejandra, about the current protests; she had joined the BLM protests in the streets of Washington, D.C., in the days following the George Floyd atrocity. She asked me what steps I was taking to center Blackness in my work and activism. I began by saying that the COVID-19 infection statistics for Latinx were as bad as those for Black people and in some cases worse. "Stop," she said to me, "that's whataboutism. Listen to yourself; we, non-Black People of Color, non-Black Latinxs, are being asked to quiet those impulses; to hear the demands in Black terms. What will YOU do differently?" In the days since we had this conversation, I have been replaying Alejandra's challenge in my mind.

A signal lesson from the BLM protests comes from the impressive role played by young people. We have seen the rise of youth who speak with clarity, vision, and vitality. Appearing on television and social media, many demonstrate the utility of critical theory, racial analyses, abolition politics, intersectional feminism, queer and trans praxis, and more. We elder LatCrits and other Race Crits can take pride in this generation; they have seized the baton; we can listen and learn from them. The present-day BLM and race movements are more racially diverse than those of the past; the many Black folks are joined by many Latinx, Asians, Indigenous people, and white accomplices.

LatCrit, as emphasized by this book's title, is dedicated to academic activism. In other words, the work of the LatCrit community—in producing knowledge, building an inclusive, supportive community for established and novice scholars, and identifying various ways of improving the material conditions of communities of color—is about breaking the grip of White Supremacy and ending all forms of racism. Yet, we must act and speak with humility and modesty; community race workers remind us of the limitations of academic activism and the constraints on scholarship. And we must speak with passion and conviction; while we have made great strides, Latinx communities are still struggling for equity, representation, recognition, and respect in many spaces. We, like other communities of color, remain at the margin of this society's imagination. With these caveats, LatCrit is an antisubordination movement and is well positioned to meet the challenges posed by the crises described below and to become one with the BLM movement's cry for justice.

Global Pandemic

COVID-19, a novel coronavirus, will have killed several hundred thousand people in the United States by the end of 2020, and BIPOC have been disproportionately affected. This pandemic, defined by the World Health Organization as the worldwide spread of a new disease, by late November 2020 infected more than sixty-two million people in every country in the globe, and one out of five of the infected are from the United States.[9] Diagnosis and recovery are fraught with difficulties, and the disease sometimes rapidly attacks multiple organs, causing a painful and frightening death. Intubated patients suffer in isolation without visitors, aided only by health providers who are gloved, robed, masked, and behind plastic shields.

Those who are suffering horrific symptoms, deprivation, and death are disproportionately families and communities of color. A few data points will show the racial disparities, even though racial data is unevenly collected by states, counties, and municipalities. Black people are dying at a rate more than 2.1 times higher than their population share; Black people are 13 percent of the U.S. population but 19 percent of deaths, where race is known (almost 46,000 Black deaths by mid-November.)[10] Because of the racial segregation in the states, compilations of county-level data are more accurate and show that, of the twenty counties with the highest death rates, in five counties Black people represent the largest racial group, and one New Mexico county is where part of the Navajo Nation is located.[11] During the period from May to August 2020, of 114,411 COVID-19-associated deaths, 24.2 percent were Hispanic/Latino and 18.7 percent were Black.[12] The causes for racial health inequities are complex, encompassing the lowly paid "essential" occupations filled by BIPOC (i.e., meatpacking, nursing home aides, cooks, and cleaners in hospitals and mortuaries), their inability to socially distance, and their use of public transportation.[13] However, one cause of poor health outcomes for BIPOC is racism—the interpersonal racial bias of health providers, the effects of stress from the intergenerational racial trauma and pervasive, quotidian abuse and humiliation they suffer, and the uneven access to health care and health insurance.[14] Structural competency is an important curricular intervention to incorporate the upstream, structural factors (including racism and racial stratification) on patient health and health care.[15]

A pandemic such as COVID-19 strips society down to basic truths, and the reasons for the racial inequities have become more obvious to the media, business executives, and policy makers. Making sense of this historic moment and innovating new analyses and solutions will be tasks for scholars in and out of the academy, especially those scholars, like LatCrits, who can adroitly imbricate race, racism, and racial power into a sustained policy agenda for change.

Economy

Unemployment filings, as of June 11, 2020, due to COVID-19 totaled a staggering 44 million,[16] and even after some rehiring, the U-6 unemployment rate, including discouraged workers, was higher than 21 percent.[17] Unemployment filings, as of October 10, 2020, had dropped to 22.6 million[18] with a U-6 unemployment rate of 12.1 in October 2020.[19] Even as jobs are added to the economy, many workers are worse off because of permanent job losses that reached almost 3 million by the end of June[20] and increased to almost 3.7 million by October 2020.[21] In the United

States, as in dozens of other countries, schools and colleges, stores, res-
taurants, recreational venues, and every sort of employment not deemed
"essential" have closed and remained in different stages of closure for
months. In March 2020, the Congress enacted legislation reaching $3
trillion to help individuals and businesses with the COVID-19 recession.[22] Economists expect the economy to shrink by 5.6 percent in 2020,
a figure that is double the contraction during the 2009 Great Recession,
but the Congress, because of Republican resistance, refused to provide
more stimulus, and millions would lose unemployment benefits during
the holidays.[23] Myriad structural and systemic choices made by policy
makers over centuries have subjected BIPOC communities to limited
access to credit and banking services, barriers to business and home
ownership, segregated neighborhoods and schools, food insecurity, and
underfunded and poorly staffed hospitals and clinics.[24] Racial justice
cannot be achieved without closing the economic gap between whites
and BIPOC, which includes paying reparations to the Black community
for the legacy of slavery, Jim Crow, and newer manifestations of those
legacies. A similar call for reparations to the Indigenous nations for the
genocide, loss of land, resources, and cultural wealth is not yet part of
the sustained national agenda for social justice transformation, nor are
other historic injustices to other communities of color yet included in
this reckoning.

Federal Government

During this catastrophic emergency, we in the United States are living
in a kakistocracy, a word I have learned only because of its pinpoint
accuracy in describing the Trump administration. A "kakistocracy"
is a system of government run by the worst, the least competent, and
most unscrupulous citizens. The Trump administration has repeatedly
shown an overt and calculated hostility through policies, programs, and
rhetoric toward people and communities of color. The confluence of
the surging pandemic, the collapse of the economy, the foreign policy

debacles, the polls favoring Democratic nominee Joe Biden's candidacy all suggest that Trump may be a one-term president. Sadly, LatCrit scholars have a treasure trove of race-inflected issues to analyze from the kakistocratic Trump regime now and retrospectively.

Climate Change

Racial justice is climate justice. As Elizabeth Yeampierre, a leader of the Climate Justice Alliance, has noted, "I can't breathe" is the BLM's tragic refrain opposing police chokeholds, but people fight for clean air because this is yet another way that their breath is taken away.[25] Communities of color are sickened by environmental racism; poor air and water quality lead to increased rates of asthma and respiratory disease. Moreover, predatory capitalism wedded to White Supremacy views communities of color as sources of disposable, low-wage labor. BIPOC communities and families suffer disproportionately from environmental hazards because of historical and contemporary racist decision makers who abandoned these communities to the worst land, dirtiest water, most polluted air, and contamination from extractive and waste disposal industries.[26]

My *Máscaras* article and the memories it evokes have become intertwined with the pandemic and my writing of this foreword. It is curious to be a scholar with an interest in masks and to live during a time when large swaths of people are obliged to don masks to minimize the spread of saliva-borne germs, especially where conforming to or protesting the masking mandate is inflected with identitarian politics. COVID-19 has disrupted all of our lives. In recent weeks, I have been sewing masks for friends and family; giving Zoom talks about CRT/LatCrit and COVID-19; homeschooling two grandkids, Marisela, age seven and Camilo, age five; working on a curriculum for training doctors about racial literacy; and inoculating myself with news reports about the spreading virus—as if I could. I have come full circle twenty-six years after writing the *Máscaras* article; I am again un/masking myself while un/braiding Latinx stories and legal discourse.

LatCrit changed my life; I credit my longevity in the academy to Lat-Crit. I cherish the friends and colleagues I have made over the twenty-some years we have been engaged in creating this architecture of people, ideas, stories, conferences, and other programs. LatCrit changed legal education by carefully opening doors for many, many People of Color interested in academia and then supporting them while they applied for jobs, learned the craft of teaching, developed a scholarly agenda, earned tenure, and were then launched into leadership positions. This book is more a journey narrative than an origin story. Yes, it is true that the need for LatCrit originated at a meeting in Puerto Rico, but the collective brilliance (if I may be so bold) of LatCrit is the journey—in the work done year after year and project after project in pursuit of a more inclusive profession and a body of knowledge that reflects the experiences and cognition of People of Color, exposes the insidiousness of racism and bigotry, and points the way to a more just tomorrow.

For those of us who for decades have been studying race, racism, and the uses and abuses of racial power, it is surprising to see the proposed social changes in response to the horrific murders of George Floyd, Breonna Taylor, Tony McDade, Ahmaud Arbery, and too many others; it is surprising because such police violence has been ignored for so long. Now more people are paying attention, businesses and other institutions are responding. We've seen the massive outpouring of support, from both BIPOC and white communities, for the idea underpinning Black Lives Matter as well as for the sporadic implementation of policies to change policing in fundamental ways. We've listened as the dominant news sources use the vocabulary associated with race scholars. Some of us have renewed hope that *this time* the attention to racial injustice will last; that *this time* the reckoning with history and the hard work of dismantling the systemic inequities, the institutional and structural forms of racism, and the everyday microaggressions will be real. There is an immediate need for the race-conscious stories, methods, and values about academic activism that form the core of the LatCrit project so eloquently described by Frank Valdes and Steven Bender in this book.

This is a propitious time for the appearance of this book. I think I speak for many when I invoke the wisdom of Malcolm X expressed in the epigraph that begins this foreword: LatCrit gave me a "we" and converted the illness of exclusion in academia into the wellness of working in a loving community for a new and better future for my grandkids and all kids. *Mil gracias* to all those who birthed and grew the LatCrit project.

Margaret E. Montoya, a founding member of LatCrit, is Professor Emerita of Law, University of New Mexico School of Law, and Visiting Professor, Department of Family & Community Medicine, University of New Mexico Health Sciences Center.

PREFACE

What is it about legal academia and even critical race theory that prevents us from even coming forward with injustice claims? What is it about the contemporary social structure of accumulation that essentially prevents this type of discussion from happening? . . . We must be vigilant as to the role of academic institutions and careerism in maintaining power relations, effected through political, economic, and social conditioning. How? . . . To begin with, we must consciously and deliberately bring to the fore and prioritize a new leadership from among those of us who are multiply marginalized—even within our own communities—in order to help us arrive at the answer.
—Sumi K. Cho

In perhaps its most simplified terms, the LatCrit experiment in critical outsider jurisprudence amounts to a multigenerational effort to organize and sustain ourselves as academic activists anchored by antisubordination values and goals. Although each and every LatCrit community member is decidedly an individual, we came and stayed together as a collective knowing we could help and benefit each other, and beyond, in principled and accountable terms. Although we occupied positions of limited privilege within the institutions that employed us, we committed and endeavored to speak—and act—from the perspective of the "bottom" of identity-based castes.

We understood that each of us, as an atomized actor, could do little to alter social or academic conditions in systemic terms. So we resolved to investigate and respect differences and to focus and build on com-monalities. We made a conscious and mutual commitment to earn trust and cultivate solidarity so that we could exert increased influence as a collective. We agreed to many phone calls, email exchanges, and meetings in order to build relationships and networks as well as to organize knowledge production events.

This emphasis on organizing academic activism and/as knowledge production runs counter to professional norms in more than one way. First, academia imagines itself insulated from the politics that bottom-up activism recognizes and exposes. Moreover, academia imagines knowledge and its production as a purely intellectual and mostly solitary exercise. Since 1995, we sensed and embraced the contrary.

The account of theory, community, and praxis we offer below in the form of an introduction, or Primer, to the LatCrit experience is our version of the result thus far. Throughout it all, we performed fully the traditional basics of our professional positions: teaching, scholarship, and service. But we infused these basics with a critical outsider bent designed to challenge and transform the status quo. And we developed initiatives that took us well beyond the call of academic duty—we prepared courses with height-ened awareness of and aims to transcend the limitations and biases of tra-ditional pedagogy, we produced scholarship with a keen appreciation of diversity and justice, and we launched academic projects that scrambled professional fault lines. Through these and other means, we organized ourselves in personal and collaborative ways to honor, deepen, and pay forward the gains of the past. Steadily and deliberately, we continually or-ganize ourselves as a diverse community to practice and foment academic activism in professional *and* social settings for the long haul.

This story of LatCrit as organized academic activism is relevant to other workers seeking to create safe zones within indifferent, if not hos-tile, industries. Though the details of context may vary greatly, indiffer-ence and hostility seem to follow similar scripts. If you are in a situation similar in any way to ours, you should care about this story because only you can pluck insights and ideas from it.

We organize ourselves specifically for academic activism because we recognize that, if we do not advocate and agitate for systemic change within the academy, nobody will—because nobody in that setting really has the interest, or the ability, to do so. Our errors and shortcomings notwithstanding, we recognize that we are uniquely situated, collectively, to improve law as a system from a critical *and* outsider perspective. In this Primer, we strive to show how our programmatic efforts and publications since 1995 provide a living example of critical outsider academics as organizers of long-term collective action, both in law and society. We hope that sharing our efforts from U.S. legal academia and elsewhere may help other persons, whomever or wherever they may be, to better organize themselves for personal yet cooperative actions.

Francisco Valdes, Miami, 2020

Steven W. Bender, Seattle, 2020

1

Background and Origins

"LatCrit"

From Naming to Doing

> From the beginning LatCrit was conceived as a community-building project focused on creating a vibrant space in which progressive scholars could and would engage in a race-conscious legal analysis of our personal reality and the multiple worlds in which we live, love, and work.
> —Margaret Montoya

Emerging from the U.S. legal academy following a 1995 colloquium in Puerto Rico on "Representing Latina/o Communities: Critical Race Theory and Practice," LatCrit theory is a genre of critical outsider jurisprudence. This contemporary scholarship includes Critical Legal Studies, Feminist Legal Theory, Critical Race Theory (CRT), Critical Race Feminism, Asian American legal scholarship, and Queer Theory, among other critical schools of legal knowledge. With that cumulative scholarly record as LatCrit's point of departure, its basic goals have been: (1) to develop a critical, activist, and interdisciplinary discourse on law and policy toward Latinas/os/x; and (2) to foster both the development of coalitional theory and practice as well as the accessibility of this knowledge to agents of social and legal transformative change. Through a variety of scholarly and activist interventions, LatCrit theorists aim to deploy Latinas/os/x' multiple internal diversities and to situate Latinas/os/x in larger intergroup frameworks, both domestically and globally, to promote social justice awareness and activism.

An important animating feature of LatCrit was the idea that these Latina/o/x "multiple internal diversities" could serve as spokes from which the entire wheel of subordination and an antisubordination movement could be built around. Rather than merely center Latinas/os/x per se as a group, the aim was to use their wide internal diversity as a way to leverage a broader way of thinking about subordination, with that thinking reflected in the considerable theory, community, and praxis that resulted. The multiple diversities within the diasporic communities called "Latina/o/x" could serve as a point of entry for programmatic studies of similar diversities—and oppressions—in "other" communities as well. We could all learn from each other while fostering a critical sense of community and solidarity along the way.

Created mostly by people of color with a decidedly critical bent and bottom-up viewpoint, LatCrit emerged and sustained itself during the height of backlash and retrenchment—in the very midst of the legal and political "counterrevolution" dedicated to rolling back legislation and doctrine from the New Deal, the Civil Rights era, and the Great Society. Within the U.S. legal academy, this "cultural" warfare has sought the intellectual liquidation of critical scholars, including bottom-up criticality.[1] Creating a collectivized base was a first step toward countering this collectivized warfare directed at us. As we discuss more fully below,[2] antisubordination values and goals thus became central to us.

Committed to the antisubordination principle from the beginning, LatCrit scholars and activists have sought to give concrete and substantive meaning to this transformative commitment. One symbolic expression of our community's dedication to the antisubordination principle is the official LatCrit logo reproduced on the book cover: a simple, stylized depiction of a globe downside up. As this logo indicates, LatCrit theorists look to the "bottom" of local and global categories to ground both theory and praxis. Building on this "bottom-up" approach of critical outsider jurisprudence, LatCrit seeks to sharpen the social relevance of critical theorizing to promote theory as a catalyst for social transformation. Formally trademarked in 2005, this group symbol not only reflects

LatCrit's specific commitment to antisubordination studies and actions but also makes a broader statement about our critical and comparative perspectives.

LatCrit theory, well into its third decade, is a still-emerging discourse that responds primarily (but not exclusively) to the long historical presence and general socio-legal invisibility of Latinas/os/x in the lands[3] now known as the United States. As with other traditionally subordinated communities within this country, the combination of longstanding occupancy and persistent marginality fueled an increasing sense of frustration among contemporary Latina/o/x legal scholars, some of whom already identified with CRT and Feminist Legal Theory by participating in and contributing to their gatherings, networks, and texts. Like other genres of critical legal scholarship, LatCrit literature reflects the conditions of its production as well as the conditioning of its early and vocal adherents.[4]

As its origins indicate, this Latina/o/x-identified genre of outsider jurisprudence was conceived as a movement closely related, especially, to CRT. Because it was born principally of the CRT experience, LatCrit theory always has viewed itself as a "close cousin" to CRT, a cousin that LatCrit always welcomes, both in spirit and in the flesh, to its gatherings.[5] But these roots included a critical assessment of CRT and other jurisprudential experiments before us (such as, for instance, legal feminism). This birthing reflected both the experiences and lessons of CRT and other precursors, as perceived by a Latina/o/x-identified sense of the mid-1990s status quo. Learning from and with the CRT workshops of previous years, we centered in LatCrit the cultivation of an open and friendly community to sustain scholars individually and collectively for the long haul.[6] LatCrit was deliberately styled as more open and inclusive than CRT—although CRT workshops at the time typically were invitation-only and limited to around thirty scholars, LatCrit conferences from the start were open to whomever registered to attend, including law students. Our first conference brought together about seventy-five participants. By the second decade, participation approached 300 attendees from around the country, hemisphere, and globe. This growth in part prompted the creation of other, smaller projects and programs described throughout this Primer.

We also wanted to affirmatively repudiate any perception or practice of elitism through a replication of the "star system" in academia.[7] Substantively, critical outsider texts, talks, and workshops during those times reflected some limitations of the "white-over-Black paradigm," which effectively narrowed analysis to those terms, and left questions about colonialism generally lingering. A group reluctance to confront "the relationship between race and sexuality"[8] also was in the air at that time. Some scholars additionally concluded that CRT, and OutCrit[9] scholarship generally, had "not adequately addressed . . . the issue of class and its relationship to race and other subordinating structures."[10] LatCrit was the beneficiary of such critiques, and CRT in turn evolved as well.[11] Though rarely comfortable, this process of learning what to do, and what to do differently, from CRT's evolution during those years "actually deepened" both CRT and LatCrit.[12]

Molded (in part) by this friendly critical assessment of the status quo within critical outsider jurisprudence and the academy at large, LatCrit theory from its very inception has been self-consciously devoted to practicing CRT's original commitments and pioneering techniques in a collectively *self*-critical way. LatCrit theorists have been determined to embrace CRT's original antisubordination vision as this movement's point of departure. Not surprisingly, then, LatCrit theory has devised a conscious and critical self-conception similar, though not identical, to CRT's.[13] From the beginning, LatCrit theorists have theorized about the purpose(s) of legal theory, and about the role of structure and substance for the community and LatCrit's intervention in light of such purpose(s).

Perhaps most notably, LatCrit conferences have been employed consciously to elucidate intra- and intergroup diversities across multiple identity axes, including those based on perspective, region, culture, and academic discipline. This expansive approach to the articulation of LatCrit theory is designed to ensure that African American, Asian

American, Native American, feminist, Queer, trans, and other OutCrit subjectivities are brought to bear on Latinas/os/x' places and prospects under the Anglocentric and heteropatriarchal rule of the United States. Though we obviously cannot train our collective attention on all diversities, issues, or contexts at once, LatCrit theorists have guided the creation of holistic theory and projects that search out and map Latina/o/x diversities and their interrelationships to unpack comprehensively and critically the complexities of Latina/o/x subordination.

Even as we were forming LatCrit and learning from CRT and feminism, we also considered the emergence of Queer scholarship at around the same time as LatCrit in the 1990s:

> Queer legal theory and LatCrit theory [came] onto the jurisprudential scene at roughly the same time—during the second half of CRT's first decade—but in markedly different ways. . . . [O]nly LatCrit theory positions itself collectively and consciously as aligned with CRT under the rubric of nonwhite outsider jurisprudence.

> . . .

> In some ways, . . . LatCrit theory may be understood as an effort to practice Queer ideals while employing CRT insights and tools; while focusing on "Latinas/os," LatCrit theory also has embraced the Queer credo of interconnected struggle as well as the CRT methods of antiessentialist community, antisubordination analysis and regular annual convocation. Though somewhat simplified, LatCrit projects and texts fairly may be viewed as a Latina/o-oriented fusion of Queer and CRT ideals and innovations, a fusion always being tested through time, experimentation and practice.[14]

Moreover, in the same way that LatCrit looked to CRT and legal feminism for lessons and insights, newer scholarly movements have looked at LatCrit and other formations to build on our collective experience. For instance, according to Athena Mutua, one of the original ClassCrits organizers, "the two models that have had the most direct impact on the evolving structure of ClassCrits have been LatCrit and the Feminism and Legal Theory Project (FLT) founded and directed by Martha Fineman. LatCrit methods, organizational format and publication mechanisms predominately informed ClassCrits' evolving and more democratic annual conference structure."[15] In addition, several of the regional people of color scholarship conferences have adopted LatCrit approaches to programmatic knowledge production and the promotion of academic activism. Snapshots like these illustrate how new genres and venues of critical outsider jurisprudence continue to emerge while building on collective experience and capture how the overlapping and expanding OutCrit formations of scholars, students, and activists continue to improve each other's lives and work.

The chapters below, in the aggregate, supply an overview of the goals, contributions, and limitations thus far of LatCrit in the interconnected spheres of theory, praxis, and the classroom—all while seeking to build community and outfit that community, structurally and interpersonally, for long-term struggle and social impact. As with LatCrit's critical but admiring assessment of CRT's substantive and structural record, this occasion presents an opportunity for critical assessment of LatCrit's own record, as well as an opportunity for community members to self-reflect on their own roles and contributions to the shared projects and aims of LatCrit as a community. As we show throughout this Primer, "LatCrit" is both a personal and a collective enterprise; its integrity, impact, and sustenance depend on both personal individual initiative as well as on collective programmatic action. This Primer is intended as a resource for those striving, as we all must, to do better.

2

Foundations

LatCrit Values and Guiding Principles

LatCrit's Guiding Principles: Grounding Solidarity

[The] expressly articulated guideposts of LatCrit have ensured that scholarly and political pursuits remain dynamic,
responsive and relevant while avoiding rigid and doctri-
naire positions. Moreover, this theoretical posture and these
guideposts have ensured that knowledge production within
LatCrit would be democratic rather than imperial. The over
two dozen LatCrit symposium issues produced over the years
are an eloquent testament to this phenomenon.
—Tayyab Mahmud

LatCrit is perhaps one of the most highly self-aware and highly theorized projects in contemporary legal discourse. A group sense of
self-awareness and criticality was manifest in LatCrit's work almost
from the outset. At the initial LatCrit Planning Retreat, held during
May 2001 in Miami, the participants developed a listing of the premises
or purposes that brought—and since then have bound—the community together. This brainstorming session asked us to distill the ideas
and ideals for which we stood as a diverse, fluid, and far-flung community of activist scholars. The resulting brief but powerful manifesto
specified ten "nonnegotiable" shared commitments as the collectivizing
foundation of LatCrit theory, community, and praxis: *intergroup justice,
antisubordination, antiessentialism, multidimensionality, praxis/solidar-
ity, community-building, critical/self-critical, ethical, transnational,* and

interdisciplinary. Reflecting on this list many years later, it is not difficult to be struck by the consistency between then and now. It is likewise quite easy to be struck by the palpable steering of the programmatic work that has followed since then—the work that took these initial thoughts and translated them, in relatively short order, into a clearer sense of the functions we impute to our work, the guideposts we need to help steer our labors in principled directions, and the postulates that we now can derive from the resulting multi-decades record of LatCrit endeavor.

Despite our many shortcomings, errors, and limitations, we have stuck as a group to these common commitments, trying always to improve our practices. In this spirit, we expand below on the four *functions* that we ascribe to antisubordination theory, and then describe seven *guideposts* we have used to theorize and act, before trying to summarize the resulting *postulates* of today as we see them. These lead to ten general *hallmarks* apparent when situating CRT/LatCrit/OutCrit scholarship within the broader framework of legal scholarship.

Functions

We began LatCrit by distilling from our intellectual ancestors' work the main functions of critical legal theorizing. We identified four functions of theory in the early days of our work together: (1) the production of knowledge; (2) the advancement of social transformation; (3) the expansion and interconnection of "different" antisubordination quests; and (4) the cultivation of critical communities and coalitions, both within and beyond the United States.[1] These four functions, we also learned, are interrelated, interactive, and interdependent.[2]

The first of the four functions—the *production of knowledge*—is a threshold belief that confirms our commitment to the production not only of "scholarship" as such but, more deeply and significantly, of the critical knowledge necessary to help fuel the social relevance of theory and theory-making.[3] Because the production of knowledge therefore is a means toward an end, the second function we identified to help us anchor our work is the *commitment not only to social relevance but also to antisubordination punch.*[4] This focus on practicality aims to produce a substantive social result—the advancement of material and structural transformation to disrupt and dismantle historical patterns of subjugation along identity lines.

To make the commitment to social transformation through knowledge production "real," we identified as the third function of our work a commitment to the *expansion and connection of antisubordination struggles*—in other words, a commitment to intersectional theory and praxis both within and beyond the United States. Our collective work always has been committed "to the notion that our theorizing, as a form of practical and transformative social struggle, must be referenced to other anti-subordination theories and struggles."[5] Our purpose therefore is not limited to self-decolonization to transcend legal and societal constraints on individuals that are emplaced through colonialism and imperialism, and maintained since, but also collectively oriented "toward a material transformation [of societies] that fosters social justice for all."[6]

The fourth function—*the cultivation of community and coalition*—also follows, and builds on, the previous ones. This function underscores that critical outsider jurisprudence must be "about more than knowledge, discourse, politics and transformation."[7] It underscores that our work must include a proactive commitment to nurturing antisubordination communities, both within and beyond academia, and within and beyond the United States. This fourth function underscores two key points: Social struggle necessarily is a cooperative endeavor, which cannot be limited to intellectual engagement; therefore, usually it takes an organized and active community to achieve enduring and meaningful progress, both in knowledge production as such and in the other three related functions sketched above.

As this synopsis makes plain, these four functions are overlapping and, ideally, mutually reinforcing. These still-controlling goals have always been interconnected so that LatCrit should never be judged on its success or failure in meeting one goal as somehow distinct or disconnected from the others.[8] Because they work best in tandem, we aim at all times to keep our eyes on each as part of the larger whole and to balance the perennial scarcity of time, energy, and other resources to help ensure the sharpest edge possible to everything we undertake.

Guideposts

To help keep us always grounded as much as possible, we distilled a set of seven guideposts from these four functions that provide more concrete markers for LatCrit's collective, ongoing work.[9] These guideposts, like the functions, emerge organically from the sum total of our collective efforts to articulate this subject position and its sense of purpose. Like the four functions above, the seven guideposts below are a reflection and projection of LatCrit theory, community, and praxis.

Rooted in our jurisprudential legacy, these guideposts emerged from the basic theoretical premises firmly established by the earlier work of legal realists and critical pioneers. For example, we accepted the premise that legal rules and actions are both manipulable and manipulated in light of their basic indeterminacy.[10] We similarly accepted that identity oftentimes plays a hidden role in the resolution of legal indeterminacy.[11] We likewise proceeded from the premise that counter-disciplinary innovations are necessary to expose and check the manipulation of law to systematically privilege some identities while subordinating other identities.[12] As with each of the above four functions, we practice these seven overlapping guideposts to the best of our personal and programmatic capacities.

We appreciate that most LatCrit community members are situated in perhaps the most legalistic country on the planet. Therefore, the first LatCrit guidepost calls upon us to *recognize and accept the inevitable political nature specific to legal scholarship in this country.*[13] This guidepost acknowledges that law is always "political" and usually ideological and that legal scholarship reflects the politics of law. Honest self-awareness of the political dimensions and ramifications of legal scholarship in this country can only sharpen our ability to employ critical theory as an engine of social justice progress.[14]

Recognizing and accepting the political nature of legal scholarship in the United States leads to the second guidepost: recognizing that *critical outsider scholars must become academic activists both within and beyond our institutions, professions, or local situations.*[15] This guidepost establishes antisubordination praxis as a framework for the connection of theory to action *and* for the interconnection of our work as teachers, scholars, and social actors. This guidepost emphasizes the relationship of our knowledge production to social action and to social justice in personal yet collective terms.

The relationship of theory to praxis, and of both to politics, inclines our work toward community and coalition-building on multiple levels and across multiple borders. The third guidepost—a proactive commitment to *building intra-Latina/o/x communities and intergroup coalitions*—channels our work toward mutual accommodation, collaboration, and transformation; it effectively inclines our programs and practices to be collaborative, open, democratic, and egalitarian.[16] This guidepost underscores specifically the importance of cooperative practices in addition to individual actions in order to advance equal justice.

To engage in this messy work of diversified community- and coalition-building, we must put in place the means to engage both "sameness" and "difference" in everything we do. Our fourth guidepost therefore became a common commitment to *finding commonalities while respecting differences.*[17] This ongoing and self-critical effort to balance both aims in everything we do, of course, does not avert controversy, but it does provide a background normative commitment to collaborative engagement and resolution of controversies in the substantive and genuine pursuit of the functions that we attribute to our collective endeavors.

To do this work—to illuminate and navigate sameness/difference divides—we must engage, in programmatic and collective terms, the many social constructions deployed to prevent a day of social justice reckoning. To do this work, we necessarily begin with the advances and accomplishments posted by previous generations of critical outsider scholars and allies. Therefore, *appreciating, incorporating, and applying the jurisprudential past to everything we undertake* became the fifth guidepost to help direct our work in the long run.[18]

To ensure this long-term grounding, we further recognized a sixth guidepost: a commitment to *continual engagement in self-critique, both individually and collectively, both in programmatic terms and otherwise.*[19] This commitment to self-criticality and self-correction helps to ensure that our efforts to "perform the theory" through the work we undertake collectively are ethical, principled, and substantively efficacious. This guidepost makes clear that the antisubordination principles and values that we profess and promote are fully applicable to our own work and choices. This guidepost also aims to ensure that our work is decolonizing, both of the self and of the larger society.[20]

Finally, our seventh guidepost calls upon us to *recognize both specificity and diversity* in the substantive construction of LatCrit theory, community, and praxis.[21] Embracing, or blending, of diversity and specificity guides our efforts toward inclusive and democratic work and helps us guard against the inadvertent indulgence of false essentialisms within or beyond Latina/o/x populations.[22] This final guidepost supplements the prior six with an explicit emphasis on the need to keep all aspects of our work self-critical as well as forward-looking, both in substance and in structure. This seventh and final guidepost reminds us continually that we must expose and resist both particularized injustice, as well as systemic patterns of injustice, as they morph over time.

Postulates

Standing back now from the sum of this work to pause and reflect on where we stand in this historical moment, we can discern four postulates derived from the collective efforts of LatCrit's initial twenty-five-plus years. The first postulate is simple: that *our shared goal is a postsubordination society.* The second postulate turns to execution: to get there from here, we need to generate *transformative change at both micro and macro levels* of human life and interaction. More specifically, the third postulate reaffirms a fundamental LatCrit belief: that we need principled and pro-active *critical coalitions* to produce antisubordination gains in both the symbolic and material aspects of transformation. The fourth postulate concludes with a similar reaffirmation of established LatCrit imperatives on accountability: that only *shared substantive principles and principled practices*, explicitly stated and self-critically applied as summarized above, can provide a sufficiently sturdy foundation for critical coalitions capable of resisting any devolution toward mere interest-convergence or similar types of rickety and often fleeting alliance.[23] All of these postulates, as well as the functions and guideposts, highlight the connection of the legal to the social and vice versa.

Hallmarks

Finally, situating LatCrit within the broader framework of outsider jurisprudence, we have identified ten key hallmarks in the body of work produced by critical scholars of color in the United States both before and since LatCrit's inception. These are: (1) the "normative bottom line" of antisubordination "values, principles, and commitments"; (2) aiming "not only to be socially relevant, but also to be transformative"; (3) "shifting the starting point of critical inquiry in ways that scramble and juxtapose mainstream or familiar categories of analysis to reveal fresh antisubordination insights and discourses"; (4) examining "issues of law or policy 'from the bottom up' of the relevant socio-legal hierarchies"; (5) deploying "doctrinal realism" that aims to expose "legal fictions that 'blind' social and legal actors"; (6) a "commitment to counter-disciplinarity in multidimensional terms"; (7) a commitment to critical historicism; (8) a commitment to social justice empiricism; (9) a commitment to local-global contextualism; and (10) a "consistent embrace of 'non-traditional' (in mainstream U.S. legal culture) methods and means for the production of legal knowledge," such as legal storytelling.[24] We outline each below.

Although the thick and rich record of critical outsider jurisprudence can be organized in different ways for different purposes, these ten key hallmarks emerge when the aim is to explore the intersection of the social and the legal in this body of scholarly work. The first hallmark signifies the normative baseline or premise of this work steeped in *antisubordination* values, principles, and commitments, while the second refers to the societal objectives of *transformation* that this work prioritizes and pursues: the express aim has been to maximize social relevance *and* impact in all scholarly choices regarding substantive priorities, research designs, and knowledge-producing methods.[25] The remaining eight hallmarks, as described in more detail below, reflect approaches or methods—the kinds of practices through which the "socio" is explored and embraced in CRT/LatCrit/OutCrit legal scholarship, both externally and internally.

The third key hallmark is the *shifting of starting points* for critical inquiry in ways that scramble and juxtapose mainstream or familiar categories of analysis to reveal fresh antisubordination insights and thereby help catalyze and inform socially transformative discourses and interventions. Frequently, this practice involves "looking to (and from) the bottom," as we note next. Significant examples of this shifting include the reframing of race (specifically, whiteness) as "property"[26] or the analysis of the unanimous *Brown v. Board of Education* rulings of the 1950s as mostly "interest convergence," and thus prone to undercutting and compromise, rather than as national enlightenment through a profound cultural shift or as justice-seeking.[27] These counter-categorical starting points bring into sharp relief how legal doctrines and fictions cover up social realities that shape the lived everyday experiences of all racialized/gendered subjects. With this shift in perspective, outsider critical inquiry works not only to produce and disseminate suppressed knowledges but also to sharpen connections to the social and foster transformative change. This resort to counter-categorical starting points of analysis oftentimes helps to reveal gaps between law and society, or the violence of the legal on the social, bringing to light areas of law or policy in sore need of repair. This methodology is one example of intellectual resistance to backlash and retrenchment.

The fourth key hallmark is an intentional examination of issues of law or policy *"from the bottom up"* of the relevant socio-legal hierarchies.[28] Applied powerfully to areas ranging from racial reparations[29] to sexual harassment,[30] this method or technique centers the social experience— and wisdom—of traditionally subordinated groups to guide the reformulation of legal doctrine or policy toward antisubordination progress. This grounding of critical perspectivity effectively centers the "socio" in all its grittiness within outsider scholarship; this particular focus aims to counteract the sanitizing abstractions of the imperial tradition within legal scholarship. Legal analysis from the bottom up, like counter-categorical starting points, scrambles both the premises and lines of inquiry in CRT/LatCrit/OutCrit scholarship to help clear the stage for socially efficacious interventions.

The fifth hallmark of this work—*doctrinal realism*—focuses squarely on the content of law, but with the aim and purpose of exposing legal fictions that blindfold social and legal actors—ranging from judges to police officers to administrators—to the intersecting social realities of identity castes. Exposing legal fictions like "reasonableness" or "neutrality" has allowed critical and allied outsider scholars to map in specific ways how law and policy engineer social injustice, including through the legal construction of formal (in)equality itself.[31] These doctrinal excavations thereby have helped to clear the way for substantive or analytical reforms better designed to ameliorate everyday injustice and promote antisubordination progress in socially relevant ways. Akin to a "bottom-up" perspective, doctrinal realism is an effort to elevate social reality and utility in the articulation of doctrine and application of policy.

The next hallmark is promotion of cross-disciplinary engagements across multiple dimensions of law, identity, and society. For instance, advancing *cross-disciplinarity* is a fundamental purpose of the LatCrit portfolio of projects, which promotes gatherings and texts that cross the borders of discipline, identity, and culture. In addition, "law and society" conferences and other "law-and" bodies of scholarship are well populated by CRT/LatCrit/OutCrit legal scholars.[32] Specific legal insights like intersectionality and antiessentialism also invite transcategorical, contextual frames of analysis.[33] Like doctrinal realism and bottom-up analysis, counter-disciplinarity can expand legal knowledge of the social dynamics that embody legal issues. This expanded knowledge can help facilitate effective antisubordination interventions and interconnections, both in law and across other disciplines.

Within the broader commitment to cross-disciplinary work, perhaps the nonlaw discipline most salient in CRT/LatCrit/OutCrit and related work is history. Without doubt, the general explanatory power of history helps to explain this centrality, especially in a body of scholarship committed to unpacking the status quo to help transform it with post-subordination vision. However, this commitment to *critical historicism* is made even more urgent and consequential by the dynamics of backlash "Kulturkampf" (cultural warfare), described in chapter 4 (note 16). As manifested in legal academia, this reaction insists on legal protection and social accommodation of "tradition"—those past practices embodying and enforcing group inequalities that the Civil War and other struggles during U.S. history have sought to amend and transcend. In practice, tradition itself is made an obstacle to change or progress— symbolically as with statues, monuments, and cultural practices celebrating inequality; materially as through false constructions of "merit" as gatekeepers; and politically as with the Electoral College system for electing the president. Therefore, the historicism manifested in CRT/LatCrit/OutCrit theorizing consistently has a decidedly critical bent—a bottom-up perspective designed to deploy historical knowledge toward understanding and dismantling the pillars and props undergirding present-day structures and dynamics of subordination. Whether unpacking the racialization of gender relations or documenting the legal construction of social whiteness, critical historicism has helped reframe knowledges of the past to better understand how to transcend continuing legacies of subordination in both law and society.[34]

The salience of critical historicism may tend to incline the CRT/LatCrit/OutCrit scholarly gaze toward the past, but OutCritical methodologies include an equally vigorous commitment to exploring present-day social realities and trends. Over the years, this commitment to *social justice empiricism* has delved into varied contexts of research, including archival investigations of case files that reveal obscured but key facts or aspects of litigations with high social impact,[35] studies of curricular/ professional conditions that aim to document institutional or social injustice or inequality,[36] and detailed fieldwork in socio- or legal trenches designed to provide empirical platforms for socio-legal analysis (as with immigration). This practice of course continues initiatives and insights from twentieth-century Legal Realists, but with an added critical edge seeking to capture contemporary social "truth" in order specifically to combat the rollback of New Deal, Civil Rights–era, and Great Society legislation[37] and, instead, build on it; in critical outsider jurisprudence, social justice empiricism is necessarily *critical*. Coupled with the commitment to critical historicism and counter-disciplinarity, this empirical commitment brings into sharper relief the tight, complex, and systemic interplay of law and society.

From our situational focus on U.S. issues we began from the beginning to resist those limitations. We endeavored to conceptualize and practice a *glocalized contextualism* that linked the local to the global, as well as to particularities and patterns. This ongoing work strives to "bring home" international rights, to bridge "domestic" and "foreign" spheres of policy and action, to infuse comparative studies with a critical sensibility, and to foster a general appreciation and embrace of internationalism in the development of critical legal scholarship.[38] This work therefore aims to document social and legal "dots" as well as to connect them; it seeks concretely and theoretically to interconnect and juxtapose both the particularities of a locality and the patterns of neoliberal globality that jointly integrate or disintegrate the social and the legal in identity-inflected policy areas ranging from governance to healthcare to trade and war. This local-global contextualism as a hallmark endeavors to apply the antisubordination normativity and social-economic ends of CRT/LatCrit/OutCrit scholarship both within and across the nation-state system.

The tenth and final hallmark of this scholarly work illustrates how critical outsider scholars engage the "socio" in their work with diverse but consistent embrace of "nontraditional" (in mainstream U.S. legal culture) methods and means for the production of legal knowledge. This endorsement and promotion of *nontraditional approaches* to legal scholarship (and education) began with the early deployment of "legal storytelling" as scholarly technique specifically within legal academia.[39] Since then, CRT/LatCrit/OutCrit methods have evolved into an array of practices and commitments sometimes described as "outsider democracy" in contrast to the "imperial scholarship" entrenched historically in mainstream norms of academic knowledge production.[40]

∗ ∗ ∗

All of these attributes—the functions, guideposts, postulates, and hallmarks—confirm a common, underlying thread: the purposeful deployment of identity and difference as assets, both intellectually and politically. The specific targets and varied forms of systemic injustice make plain that identities like race, sex, and class matter today differently, but no less than, in 1954 when *Brown* was decided. If social identities are to matter, they should matter for the better.

A review of LatCrit programs in the chapters that follow, and of the appendices to this text, attests to the collective practice of our commitments in the form of the functions, guideposts, postulates, and hallmarks presented above. Grounded in the core values of antisubordination and democracy,[41] these ideas and practices marshal the power of our multiple differences and diversities to produce critical insights about law and about society. Applied critically and self-critically, these fundamentals support academic activism in both law and society.

The Antisubordination Principle/Value: Our Normative Anchor

Understand that the histories and legacies of multiple subordinations in this country, and their historic and current
interconnection with globalized neocolonial systems of subordination, also can affect your mistreatment in manifold,
and sometimes in as-yet undetected, ways.
—Jerome M. Culp, Jr., Angela P. Harris & Francisco Valdes[42]

The antisubordination principle that undergirds much of the LatCrit
project is generally associated with critical outsider jurisprudence,
although its initial articulation originates with Owen Fiss.[43] In both its
original articulation and its subsequent OutCrit elaboration, the antisubordination principle is conceived as a jurisprudential honing of the
antidiscrimination principle in order to "get at" the social problems
associated with domination and subjugation.[44] The antidiscrimination
principle, as interpreted judicially in the form of formal equality, looks
only to whether a plaintiff can produce "smoking gun" evidence showing that the defendant individually, consciously, and overtly "intended"
to discriminate against the plaintiff as an individual. This narrowly
contrived approach ignores the known problems of pretextual discrimination and the use of proxies, both of which can be used easily—and
have been used historically—to disguise intentional discrimination.
Similarly, this doctrinal setup also declares evident discriminatory
effects to be mostly irrelevant; legally, only judicial characterizations of
"purpose" matter in the end. This judicial framing of the antidiscrimination principle emplaces within formal equality an undue gauntlet of
evidentiary hurdles that tends to exculpate discrimination and reinforce
inequality.

This doctrinal regime also disregards the social positions and asymmetries of "different" actors. It equates whites with Blacks, and men with
women, as if persons in each group within the pairs shared a similar
history and social position of equality already. In social and legal fact,

whites and men as groups have always enjoyed positions of systemic power and privilege; they have never encountered systemic blocks against their right to vote, to education, to own property, to serve as jurors, to be licensed as lawyers, or to any other social goods. Whites and men have always been in charge.

Meanwhile, due to invidious discrimination—whether de jure or considered "de facto"—both Blacks and women (and many others) have been subjected to systemic exclusion and disempowerment—even enslavement. In contrast to whites and men, Blacks and women systematically have been denied all of the above rights for decades, if not centuries. The two groups in each pair obviously are not on level terms even today: they most certainly are not "similarly situated." Decreeing them so in the abstract is a legal fiction that betrays equality and prevents solutions to persistent social problems like poverty, violence, and exploitation.

Nonetheless, under the blindfolding formalism of antidiscrimination doctrine, judges treat both groups in each pair as if they are similarly situated. Antidiscrimination doctrine blindfolds law to the difference between systemic privilege and systemic subordination; it ignores the difference between preserving castes and upholding equal justice for all. It pretends all identity groups are similarly situated already and that individuals can be routinely atomized and severed from their groups in solving the collectivized social-legal problems of systemic inequality.

Through this skewed judicial construction, equality law was made "blind" to the social and conceptual asymmetries between *in*groups and *out*groups, as well as the persons categorized by them. On this basis, judges started applying the antidiscrimination principle as if all kinds of discrimination are the same and equally suspect. In particular, this construction failed, by design, to distinguish between *remedial* and *invidious* forms of discrimination.

This equation in turn enabled judicial notions of "reverse discrimination" to halt race-conscious remedies for invidious discrimination, such as affirmative action programs enacted by democratic means. Under the antidiscrimination principle as enforced by judicial decree, remedies to discrimination were transmuted into a new kind of discrimination; the democratic remedy to invidious discrimination became the new judicial problem to be confronted and often undone.[45] Nevertheless, history shows that the systemic problem was and is collectivized subordination; any principled, good-faith cure to inequality and its social problems must therefore be tailored in fact to collectivized antisubordination purposes.[46] Otherwise, as continues to be the case with antidiscrimination law, pervasive group inequalities and social problems will fester despite professed commitments to equal justice.

A key problem with antidiscrimination as an approach to equal justice is that it is designed to protect and project the "illusion of individualism" that pervades and distorts the entire system to justify collectivized injustice.[47] Judicial doctrines that demand individualized claims, analysis, and remedies create and perpetuate a mismatch between actual problems and potential solutions; these doctrines demand abstracted, decontextualized claims, analyses, doctrines, and outputs. This mismatch ensures that allowed remedies never match the injury, entrenching in law and society the cumulative, continuing injustice of entrenched caste systems. Within this system, the idealized "appeal of the antidiscrimination principle may be nothing more than an illusion."[48]

Through early critiques of antidiscrimination and its fictions, legal scholars and advocates began to discuss an alternative grounded in the documented realities that pervade life at the "bottom" of identity-based castes. The "antisubordination principle" that emerged came to emphasize a twin focus: first, a focus on the pervasive, collective, and cumulative effects of caste systems; and, second, a focus on the identity groups actually subordinated by them in social, economic, and legal terms. This approach, embraced as a foundational principle by LatCrit, aimed to displace legal fictions and formalism with social reality more honestly consistent with the equality commitments expressed through the Fourteenth Amendment and cascades of U.S. civil rights legislation.

In short, judicial fashioning of antidiscrimination doctrine focuses on individuals as social atoms and declares the group nature of systemic injustice to be anomalous or "irrelevant," whereas antisubordination frameworks put groups created since colonialism at the center of legal analysis and remedial responses. These bottom-up frameworks recognize the distinction between privilege and subordination and that, in fact, subordination is not an equally distributed social condition. They emphasize that collectivized subordination, not discrimination as such, is the problem facing individual members of historically and currently disempowered groups. As Jerome Culp, Jr., Angela Harris, and Francisco Valdes noted:

> Critical race theorists therefore start with a different problem: not whether discrimination is taking place in contemporary society, but what it is like to have as part of one's everyday experience the possibility that one is the target of discrimination—the possibility, that is, of becoming without warning the victim of "spirit murder." . . . To be part of a pattern of discrimination that we can "prove" at the aggregate level but never at the individual level is to be a subject the truth of whose experience is always in doubt. For critical race theory, this analytical structure is the Catch-22 of prevalent forms of antidiscrimination discourse.
>
> . . .
>
> [T]he traditional legal model . . . say[s] to individuals at risk everywhere, "Accept the risks of the system and assume justice unless you can prove 'discrimination' either through overwhelming statistical evidence or the smoking gun of subjective intent." Critical race theory says, "Assume the opposite: Unless the system proves it is not subject to or complicit in entrenched structures of subordination, trust no one and question everything."[49]

In social and economic effect, the antidiscrimination principle expresses the perspective, and collectivized interests, from above, whereas the antisubordination principle expresses the perspective, and collectivized interests, from below. LatCrit scholars and projects thus appreciate how the antisubordination principle and values are more consistent with equality and—more specifically—with the social and legal goals of critical theory in pursuit of equal justice for all. Indeed, this antisubordination perspective shows more fidelity to the final text and principal purposes of the proequality Fourteenth Amendment than does the judicial design of antidiscrimination fictions and doctrines.

This antisubordination approach recognizes that the principal intent and purpose of the Fourteenth Amendment was to dismantle collectivized patterns and practices of caste and supremacy. Although subordination (like privilege) is experienced by individuals, it is systemically imposed based on actual or perceived membership in some identity-based social group. Blacks are subordinated because they are Black; women because they are women: association or identification with the already-subordinated group is what makes those individuals targets of discrimination. The antisubordination aims of the Fourteenth Amendment therefore focused intentionally on groups—specifically whites and Blacks—organized by law into castes, not (just) on individuals as atomized, free-floating targets of subordination (or privilege). As judicially designed, antidiscrimination law bifurcates the individual from the group and thus subverts the remedial intentions of those who drafted and ratified the Fourteenth Amendment. In this way, antidiscrimination law impedes transformative equality reforms and preserves systems of identity castes.

From this LatCrit perspective, dominant versions of equality jurisprudence serve as disguises that knowingly legitimate persistent patterns of group inequalities correlated for generations to social identities. By design, dominant doctrine proclaims one thing but produces the contrary. Perversely, it subverts equality in law and society under the very banner of the Fourteenth Amendment.

To avoid replicating this dynamic, LatCrit and OutCrit scholars have also embraced and applied the insights of antiessentialism and intersectionality in conjunction with antisubordination. Both of these insights provide analytical tools that enable more precise understandings of social groups and social problems. Each aims to incorporate differences within groups to design antisubordination knowledge and action; for instance, not all Latinas/os/x are Roman Catholics or immigrants, even though they commonly may be thought to be so.

Generally, "essentialism" is a label applied to claims that a particular perspective reflects the common experiences and interests of a broader group, as when working-class men purport to define the class interests of "workers," or white women purport to define the interests of all "women," without acknowledging intragroup differences of position and perspective—differences that can produce consequences for lawmaking and policy-making decisions. Essentialist categories oftentimes divert or inhibit attention to intragroup differences, helping to consolidate a group's agenda around the group's internal elites.[50] In contrast, antiessentialism seeks to reveal intragroup differences to resist relations of subordination and domination that may exist within and among the members of any particular group. Therefore, "[a]ntisubordination principles and analysis, applied in critical and self-critical ways, provide the substantive limits for and directions of antiessentialism in LatCrit theory, community, and praxis. Thus, antiessentialism is no end unto itself; its utility is defined in relation to a contextual antisubordination purpose. In LatCrit theory, community and praxis, antisubordination ideally always contextualizes and informs antiessentialism."[51] In LatCrit practice, the former anchors the latter.

Intersectionality similarly emphasizes the complexity of group identities. Intersectional analysis calls for attention to multiple axes of identity within a given antisubordination framework.[52] Intersectionality emphasizes that each and every individual simultaneously embodies multiple identities—race, sex, orientation, class, religion, nationality, and more—and that different combinations of those identities call for different analyses or policies. For instance, a wealthy or urban woman is more likely to have the means and proximity to exercise her formal right to reproductive choice despite the legal and practical obstacles placed in her way, whereas poor or rural women are less able to overcome the same roadblocks. Due to intersectional differences, not all women (or men)—whether cis or trans—are similar, or similarly situated, in relationship to privilege and subordination.

Thus, antisubordination is not a stand-alone commitment. In Lat-Crit theory and praxis, it grounds our uses of antiessentialism and intersectionality. These three values—principles, insights, and tools— are interdependent and indivisible: antisubordination helps to ensure principled, bottom-up applications of antiessentialist and intersectional knowledge.

3

LatCrit Contributions to OutCrit Jurisprudence

Five Substantive Highlights

Critical Knowledge and Knowledge Production

> LatCrit provides space for me to continue to examine my
> own whiteness and to deepen my commitments to disman-
> tling white colonial supremacy. LatCrit centers race, and I,
> as a white person, participate in LatCrit in an effort to con-
> stantly listen, observe, and learn, as I deepen my solidarity
> and my praxis. . . . On my best days, LatCrit is the space that
> keeps me honest and draws my work deeper in its commit-
> ments to the praxis of antisubordination work.
> —Shelley Cavalieri

Intellectually, the LatCrit experiment proceeded from the substantive
and methodological baselines established principally by CRT and legal
feminism in the United States. We proceeded from the understanding
that identity is always a constitutive, though sometimes hidden, element
of law and policy and that multiple identities are always implicated in
the adoption of any particular legal or policy regime.[1] We acknowledged the centrality and relevance of "difference" in the understanding
of the multiple identities embodied by all individuals and present in
every social group.[2] As indicated above by the opening quote, we managed inclusively the engagement of whiteness as a cultural and legal
category, within both the academy and society.[3] We embraced the antisubordination principle as a normative anchor that shows fidelity to

the Fourteenth Amendment. We took up the ongoing interrogation of existing socio-legal identities, as constructed over time, to pursue the insights of intersectionality, antiessentialism, and multidimensionality.[4] We accepted that social justice, in the form of social transformation, was the ultimate marker of relevance in the articulation of theory and the production of knowledge. In short, we took the substantive insights and gains of OutCrit theorizing as they stood at that time[5] and endeavored to both develop and apply them in light of the limitations or shortcomings suggested by our jurisprudential experiences to date. From the substantive baseline formed by these and similar insights of critical outsider jurisprudence up to the mid-1990s, the LatCrit community proceeded to make its own intellectual contributions in the ongoing elaboration of outsider scholarship from within (and from without) the U.S. legal academy.

These intellectual contributions may be framed in a number of different ways and levels of description. However, the five substantive contributions detailed below are among the most significant thus far. Of these, perhaps the single-most significant theoretical contribution of LatCrit scholarship specifically since its inception in the mid-1990s has been the centering and elaboration of Latina/o/x identity in U.S. law and society in explicitly non- or de-essentialized terms.[6] As discussed here, these analyses and projects have encompassed both intragroup and intergroup issues. This inclusive, expansive approach aims to cultivate cross-group frameworks of analysis designed to produce not only knowledge but also coalitional methods and theories. These approaches in turn have led to counter-disciplinary and internationalist emphases in LatCrit projects and discourses to transcend "domestic" constructions of race, ethnicity, and other categories of identity relevant to law and policy. Finally, LatCrit theorists have insisted that "class" and other categories of identity must be understood as interrelated and interlocking rather than as different or disconnected elements of socio-legal regulation. These collective investigations have demonstrated the rich diversity of Latina/o/x communities in the United States, showcasing complexities not only in terms of race and ethnicity but also in terms of religion, culture, language, sexuality, imperialism, and colonialism.[7] These investigations represent personal and cooperative efforts to practice shared commitments across multiple sources of difference—personal, cultural, institutional, professional, and otherwise.

LatCrit added the race question on my intellectual and political agenda. Weaned as a post-colonial Marxist, not surprisingly the class question, praetorianism and imperialism demarcated my canvas of intellectual engagements. Becoming LatCrit induced me instantly to explore the constitutive role of colonialism in modern construction of race and the enduring operations of race in conditions of post-coloniality. . . . LatCrit also put the Latina/o question on my plate. . . . The Latinx question also engendered a more comprehensive and nuanced reading of an always unstable, always shifting assemblage of the very concept of race, particularly in post-"discovery" Americas. . . . Henceforth, one could not speak about race, in the Americas or otherwise, without taking account of modernity, colonial history, post-coloniality, culture, language, religion, hybridity, patterns of arrival, changing labor markets, gender, sexuality, etc.
—Tayyab Mahmud[8]

Latina/o/x Identities and Diversities[9]

Latinas/os are not exempt from the oppression of White supremacy, yet, as a group or individually, we often are seduced into thinking we are White. . . .

Latinas/os must investigate the position of the Latina/o group within the Black-White paradigm and the racial hierarchy constructed thereon, as well as investigate the manipulation of our group's racial identity. This effort and a unified

front of communities of color and allied groups can result in
a transformation of equal protection jurisprudence and antidiscrimination law.

—Enid Trucios-Haynes[10]

The first of the significant LatCrit contributions we address is the
scholarly elaboration of "Latina/o/x" identity as a multiply variegated
category.[11] To do so, we embarked on collective and programmatic
investigations of ethnicity, religion, language, immigration, and similar constructs to better understand, and to underscore, the intragroup
diversities of "Latina/o/x" populations, specifically, but not only, in the
United States.[12] These collective investigations not only sparked vigorous
debate and searching inquiry but also exposed the fallacy of the "essentialized" Latina/o/x employed in mainstream venues to make law and
policy regarding Latinas/os/x.[13] These investigations demonstrated and
documented key demographic facts, including that not all Latinas/os/x
are Hispanic; that not all Latinas/os/x are Roman Catholic; that not all
Latinas/os/x speak Spanish or want to; and that not all Latinas/os/x who
want to live or work in the United States can do so due to immigration
restrictions. Conversely, these investigations showcased the complexities
and diversities of Latina/o/x communities in terms of race and ethnicity,[14] religion,[15] culture,[16] imperialism and colonialism,[17] language and
its suppression,[18] class,[19] and immigration status.[20] These overlapping
inquiries showcased "Latina/o/x" people as fluid, multiply diverse diasporas born of settler colonialism and imperial identity politics. These
investigations, in short, de-centered uncritical assumptions that all Lati-
nas/os/x fit predominant stereotypes—assumptions that skew law and
policy to the detriment of multiply diverse Latina/o/x communities.

Intra/Inter-Group Frameworks

[We] have sought to situate LatCrit analysis of the Latina/o
condition in intergroup social frameworks and crossgroup

historical contexts that take into account both the present
and the past in the delineation of LatCrit priorities and projects. This intergroup framing expands the circle of perspectives brought to bear on the Latina/o condition and deepens
the substance of LatCrit discourse. The diversity of position
and perspective enabled by this intergroup discourse ensures
a broadly inclusive multilateral dialogue that listens both to
Latina/o experiences and to others as well. In this way, Lat-
Crit theory is informed by diverse "outside" viewpoints-in
addition to diverse "internal" viewpoints. This openness to
both "internal" and "external" critique helps to ensure a critical (as well as self-critical) approach to Latina/o interests and
issues. In this way, LatCrit scholars learn from—and teach
each other—about the similarities and differences that construct domination and subordination across multiple vectors
of experience and identity, both within and beyond Latina/o
contexts.

—Elizabeth M. Iglesias & Francisco Valdes[21]

LatCrit theorists have sought to advance critical outsider jurisprudence
by developing and calling for analyses and projects that encompass both
intragroup and intergroup issues—in other words, analyses and projects
that promote both intra- and intergroup understanding. This approach
to scope has facilitated a more detailed and accurate mapping of the patterns formed across groups by the particularities reflected in each and
invited comparative, intergroup study of common categories like "race"
or "ethnicity" or "culture" that are relevant to the subordination of "different" social groups. Over time, this effort has helped produce a better
comprehension and critique of the interlocking nature of the "different"
systems of subordination that jointly and severally keep existing hierarchies of injustice and inequality in place both within and across social
groups. Using programmatic methods such as those discussed in the
next chapter, we effectively employed LatCrit and Latina/o/x diversities

as a kind of spoke around which the wheel of subordination could be mapped and an antisubordination coalition built.

Antisubordination Internationalism and Critical Comparativism

> LatCrit theorists must seek to forge an identity that embraces differences and change in order to confront a world that is involved in an attempt to eliminate difference. What this means, inter alia, is that a LatCrit perspective must be sensitive to the dangers of all universalizing rhetoric. Attempts at setting international standards, for instance, must be viewed with a degree of skepticism. Whose values should such standards reflect? Who is to benefit from the harmonization of legal regimes? Should we really be engaged in the popular project of exporting our environmental standards, rules, regulations, and institutions, for wholesale adoption, to other states? . . .
>
> [W]e must resist the simple attempt at imposing our own standards on others and resist the trend towards homogenization of human diversity, which seems to follow so naturally from the moment of globalization in which we are told we exist.
>
> —Ileana Porras[22]

In addition, LatCrit theorists have contributed a newfound emphasis on internationalism and transnationality in the ongoing evolution of critical outsider jurisprudence. Transcending "domestic" constructions of race, ethnicity, and other identity-based categories relevant to law and policy, this expansion and comparativism have helped to deepen and broaden critical understanding of those categories as exercises of power. They also have helped expose how those "different" exercises of power, using the "same" categories, are tailored in myriad ways to local circumstances and varied regions or locales.[23] This third contribution—akin to the effort to examine law and power in cross-group contexts—has helped bridge what used to be a gulf between the "local" or "domestic" and the "global" or "foreign" in both law generally and also in critical outsider jurisprudence.

Counter-disciplinarity

Critical race scholars and LatCritters have employed the teachings of psychology to inform our understanding of the operation and consequences of unconscious racism and stigma. From sociology we have gained an appreciation of microaggressions and the consequences of culture. The use of constructs from other disciplines has also contributed to our understanding the processes of subordination, both explicit and implicit. . . .

[But] [o]ur appropriate distrust of the tools and policy instruments of economic orthodoxy ha[s] limited our ability to do what must be done to eliminate the ideologies and instrumentalities of subordination from this society. . . . If LatCrit and critical race theory are to create lasting change reaching to the heart and roots of the subordination project they must overcome their resistance to economic analyses as a mode of interdisciplinarity.

—Charles R. P. Pouncy[24]

The fourth contribution we have endeavored to make to the broader project of critical outsider jurisprudence is to push for greater interdisciplinary,[25] or counter-disciplinary, texts, projects, and programs. This emphasis on inter- or counter-disciplinarity, like the cross-group and internationalist initiatives, aims to refine and develop the core hallmarks or concepts of critical outsider jurisprudence as previously mapped out in chapter 2. The hope is that all disciplines progressively learn more and better from all other disciplines. The proactive effort to make other disciplines integral to the elaboration of LatCrit theory specifically, while not always successful, has helped both to bolster and to texture our understandings of and approaches to identity as a legal tool; we understand better how "different" identities are being manipulated for particular purposes in particular places at particular times and, in light of that understanding, how to use identities as assets in antisubordination struggles.

Class and (Not or) Identity

> That racism can be addressed without addressing the economic class configurations that structure race is doubtful. Similarly, the kind of mass movement needed to challenge dominant—economic-class power would require dealing with the racial issues that divide those who must work for their living as opposed to those, along with those with specialized skills, who live off the work of others.
> —Athena D. Mutua[26]

Finally, the fifth basic contribution in this brief sketch is the collective or programmatic insistence that "class" and "identity" are *not* oppositional categories of analysis and action and, instead, must be understood as "different" dimensions of the interlocking systems of oppression always under interrogation.[27] This approach, in other words, emphasizes that "class" is, itself, an axis of socio-legal identity and that, as such, it must be incorporated into intersectional analyses of power in law and society. In LatCrit scholarship this approach has tempered the influence of dichotomies between "discursive" and "material" aspects of power based on social identities[28] and has positioned us to better understand how class and other forms of identity are mutually constitutive and mutually reinforcing, both in law and in society.

Influenced by LatCrit contributions to critical outsider jurisprudence, as well as those from other critical scholarly communities such as critical feminism, queer theory, and CRT, ClassCrits was formed in 2007 as a critical scholarly community centering class within OutCrit analysis. Designed to tackle a gap in antisubordination consciousness and praxis, this new scholarly formation "focuses on the interplay of law and socio-economic stratification, and on the interaction of socio-economics with other axes of identity, like race, gender, disability or sexual orientation."[29] LatCrit "methods, organizational format and publication mechanisms predominately informed" ClassCrits' structure, with outcomes thus far that "both reflect and go beyond the LatCrit example."[30]

* * *

LatCrit's blending of substance and method consistently has emphasized intersectional analyses, collaborative action, long-term planning, international frameworks, and a continual fusion of theory and action. Over time, the intellectual commitments and programmatic initiatives of the LatCrit/OutCrit community have given rise to a form of critical "outsider democracy" as a viable, activist alternative to the imperial tradition of legal knowledge production and education.[31] This blending of substance and method steadily has emphasized and advanced community-building, institution-building, and programmatic autonomy as personal and collective praxis.

Today, CRT/LatCrit/OutCrit scholars continue this individual and programmatic work with a focus on current or emerging issues. In recent years, for example, outsider scholars have examined the interplay of poverty and globalization and how these phenomena correlate to race, ethnicity, gender, and other socio-legal identity categories transnationally.[32] Similarly, these critical networks of scholars have engaged arguments about "color blindness"[33] and "post-racialism"[34] or similar racial justice issues that emerged in the late 1990s and early 2000s. The exploration of these frontiers—in tandem with the ongoing work of the past several decades—constitutes a key part of the CRT/LatCrit/OutCrit research agenda today.

4

Community and Method

Building Zones of Critical Safety

Nurturing Groupness: Rotating Centers, Shifting Bottoms, and Streams of Programming

> "What group should be at the center of a given study or en-
> terprise?" Whose "faces are at the bottom of the well;" and,
> "What model shall we use to analyze a given situation?"
> —Athena D. Mutua

LatCrit's approach consciously is designed not only to center Latinas/
os/x in a manner that minimizes privileging any one Latina/o/x identity
or interest over another but also to ensure critical discussion of Latinas/
os/x as part of the larger intra- and intergroup schematics formed in part
through colonialism, capitalism, and law. This LatCrit drive for diversity and particularity aims to create an intellectual and social culture
enabling the LatCrit community collectively to overcome essentialisms
of Latinas/os/x and other groups, which sometimes stand in the way of
critical outgroup and OutCrit coalitions. This incremental critical effort
is intended to promote and ground intra- and intergroup antisubordination coalitions by ensuring the representation and investigation within
the LatCrit community of various power hierarchies and their mutually
reinforcing interplay.

In practice, this constant and perpetual balancing of similarities and
specificities produces a "rotation of centers." At each gathering, LatCrit
programs have allocated time and prominence to intersectional issues in
a manner that in effect rotates the "center" of LatCrit discourse among

various, and sometimes overlapping, intra- and intergroup concerns. This rotational practice effectively requires all participants to "de-center" from time to time salient identities or preferred issues to juggle our collective limited resources. The joint objective every time, and also over the years, remains constant, even while sites and centers rotate: to incorporate as fully as possible in all LatCrit programs, as well as in the overall LatCrit record, the manifold intra-Latina/o/x diversities and intergroup issues that affect antisubordination quests, including those of Latinas/os/x. If assessed critically and pragmatically, and if managed democratically, this communal process of continual and rotational analysis is the best—if not the only—route to balancing and expanding from year to year the programmatic attention given to these intricate issues, and to their complex interrelationship, in light of the discursive demands established by postmodern, intersectional insights.

Complementing the programmatic innovations of LatCrit conferences around "rotating centers" is the conception of "shifting bottoms"[1] to recognize and center diverse marginalities in principled and ethical ways at different times and over time. Combining rotating centers and shifting bottoms provides a conceptual and planning framework for situating "different" social problems or populations at the center of our programmatic inquiries. In this way, diversely situated individuals and groups can and should take lead roles in exposing and combatting interlocking systems of injustice, recognizing that, depending on circumstances, a "different" outsider community might find itself "at the bottom"—as well as sometimes at the center.[2] In coining the concept of shifting bottoms, LatCrit scholar Athena Mutua supplied the following illustration in the context of language supremacy and subordination:

> [Despite occupying the bottom of the racial hierarchy,] Blacks likely are not on the "bottom" with regard to language oppression within the United States. . . . Instead, it appears Latinos/as are on the "bottom" because they embody, so to speak, a shared language uniting them that is

the object of White Power's obsession. . . . Here, White Power's obsession is either with brown bodies or the Spanish language; black bodies have little to do with it as a distraction or fundamental point. In this country, Spanish translates to a central site or category of oppression, thereby relegating its speakers to the metaphorical "bottom" of this society in those specific terms.

. . . [H]istorically, white society has discriminated against Latinos/as on the basis of the Spanish language. . . .

. . . Spanish spoken in the United States challenges White Power's conception of itself and its social goals in two significant ways. First, the increasing numbers of Latinos/as portend significant political power for a group that speaks a language other than English. This threatens White Power's mythical vision of a solitary nation united around one language, occupied by one people descended from the same ancestor. Second, Spanish is associated with a racialized group and culture. . . .

[Today,] the "English Only" Movement is both a sign of White Power's movement to institutionalize its social vision of America, and of White Power's increasing obsession. . . . In trying to eliminate Spanish as a basis of cohesion for the Latino/a community, while simultaneously limiting their participation in American society, White Power is reinforced and its cultural hegemony left firmly intact.

[In sum,] the "bottom" metaphor leads us to the idea that the groups represented at the "bottom" shift, depending on the issue and circumstance. The shifting "bottom" directs us to shift our focus, shift our thinking, and perhaps shift our analytical tools when we are trying to understand the experiences of different groups. It instructs us to look specifically at how different groups and issues are constructed and experienced both in similar and dissimilar ways. This essay suggests that although Blacks are at the bottom of a colorized racial hierarchy, Latino/as are at the bottom of a racialized language hierarchy, at a minimum, and perhaps at the bottom of a racial system marked by the Spanish language, among other things. The "bottom" has indeed shifted.[3]

This programmatic framing of shifting bottoms is a reminder that history, politics, and context define and determine the "bottom"—as well as the demands of equal justice praxis grounded in this recognition.

In addition to providing theoretical insight and operational grounding, LatCrit innovations like rotating centers and shifting bottoms have led to institutional practices that promote organic developments in the pursuit of critical knowledge and coalitional community as justice. Institutionally, LatCrit conferences and colloquia have remained notably mobile in their substance and form during more than two decades—flexible, varied, and shifting. This mobility is fueled in great part by the careful and conscious showcasing of new generations in programs, publications, and projects, but this fluidity is also contoured by a constant and conscious effort to calibrate expansion *and* continuity. Our programmatic goal is to engineer a shared, cross-group, transgenerational sense of progression through "streams of programming" that also help to develop our shared understanding of specific topics. These streams of programming are designed as a substantive and collective progression of understanding based on knowledge and experience that can lead to ever more collaborative and effective action against the systemic legacies of identity politics, both within the legal academy and throughout society.

In practice, these streams comprise a series of events over the course of several consecutive years spotlighting a particular issue or topic to ensure a community-wide awareness of them in ways that one-time events are unlikely to achieve. Based on ongoing experience, we use different formats to carry out these extended programmatic lines of inquiry. Depending on the topic or circumstance, we might start with conference plenary events and follow up with smaller-scale, even informal, gatherings ranging from workshops, panels, and presentations to special retreats or vice versa. Over the years, these streams advanced shared knowledge and personal relationships throughout various intellectual networks. Combining rotating centers focused on shifting bottoms with streams of programming slowly but steadily invited a sharing environment of knowledge, understanding, and solidarity.

Embracing Difference: The Diverse Reach of LatCrit Networks

[H]ow do we deal with each other? How do we as African-
Americans, we as White-Americans, we as Asian-Americans,
we as Latino/Latina Americans participate together in struggles that involve people who are not ourselves?
—Jerome M. Culp, Jr.[4]

From the beginning, LatCrit theorists embraced productive tensions
based, first, on identity-related sources of "difference" (both within and
beyond the Latina/o/x population) and, second, on the collective decision to construct an "open" space in LatCrit programs and venues. The
most common early expression of these productive tensions focused on
the relevance of "race" to Latina/o/x populations, to which we turned
our attention in the first couple of years.[5] More particularly, the question that oftentimes arose focused on the role and relevance of groups
or communities racialized and/or ethnicized as something other than
"Latina/o/x"—and whether scholars who identify with such communities are within the scope of LatCrit inquiry and community membership.

In other words, this question or tension asks whether scholars or
projects not conceived of as "Latina/o/x" in some essentialized or essentializing way are, or can be, part of the LatCrit whole. Our collective and programmatic engagement of this particular productive
tension thus focused on the racial and other diversities within and
across Latina/o/x communities, especially in the United States, to underscore commonalities that otherwise might be overlooked. This approach sought to de-center the essential Latina/o/x and to showcase
intra-Latina/o/x diversities, illustrating concretely how constructs like
"race" are as relevant to "Latina/o/x" interests as to other racialized
social groups. In effect, this approach provides a substantive and theoretical response to several related queries: "Do Black people belong in
LatCrit?" or "Do Asian people belong in LatCrit?" or "Do white people
belong in LatCrit?" or even "Do Indigenous people belong in LatCrit?"

Responding affirmatively in each instance, this approach has sought to emphasize that Latina/o/x populations embody all racial (and other identity) categories; racial difference is already an intra-Latina/o/x reality, and intergroup inquiries can only illuminate how race operates in law and society.

In this way, we endeavored to demonstrate why and how the study of all racial categories by scholars with "different" racial subject positions is necessarily integral to a holistic and incisive LatCrit analysis of identity as law and power. Through this approach we have sought both to keep the "Lat" in LatCrit theory while simultaneously making the case for the necessary inclusion of diverse viewpoints in the elaboration of all genres of critical outsider jurisprudence. This, then, in the words of the late LatCrit pioneer Jerome Culp, Jr., is how we "participate together in struggles that involve people who are not ourselves."

This query is central and perennial. It is the challenge of principled praxis in and through critical coalitions. It is a call to solidarity across difference, which is indispensable to transformative progress and systemic justice. LatCrit's ethos of embracing "difference" has countered the top-down framing of "identity politics" designed to suppress the capacity of advocates and groups to use shared identity-based grievances as points of coalescence and organization. Rather, LatCrit as a community appreciates how subordinated social identities can mobilize individuals into action-oriented groups—rather than divide them—and thus are key to equal justice struggles. For these reasons, LatCrit efforts always have, and still do, aim proactively to include people who are not ourselves in all that we plan or do.

Our programs and projects since 1995 show this inclusivity is not limited to questions of race or ethnicity. Instead, we have deployed the three community methods noted above—rotating centers, shifting bottoms, and streams of programming—to explore multiple intersections of gender, class, religion, sexuality, immigration status, and other identity-making markers. This intra-/inter- group exploration of difference and diversity confirms that Latinas/os/x, like members of other social groups, are not the "same" but nonetheless share important histories and legacies.

Over the years, this continual grappling with difference has slowly but steadily expanded the diversity and reach of LatCrit labors and networks. Embracing our diversities while respecting them as differences has allowed us to navigate internal conflicts while continuing our collective work. Sticking mutually to our commitments, functions, guideposts, postulates, and hallmarks—especially when hard or messy to do so—has shown us that tension and disagreement can be made into opportunities for building strength and trust for the longer term. Rather than avoid conflict, when it erupts, we try to make it an opportunity to build solidarity.

Beyond the Imperial Scholar: LatCrit's "Democratic" (or "Big Tent") Model

[LatCrit] connected me to a group of people who shared some of my own passions and motivations for being in legal academy. It was a broad antisubordination agenda, not one strictly limited to race or strictly limited to gender or only class or only sexual orientation, but an ability to perceive problems in a much more holistic manner. That's what I wanted because it was a place where everyone was welcome regardless of what particular focus their own scholarly projects took. It was that inclusiveness, [that] openness to a variety of perspectives that to me was so significant. It created a home for me.

—Carmen Gonzalez[6]

LatCrit commitments include ensuring nonhierarchical arrangements in everything we undertake, encompassing an explicit commitment to avoiding "star system" practices in our programmatic approach to knowledge production and community engagement. Our commitments to mentor and feature rising generations and against star-system practices amount to a repudiation of longstanding "imperial" academic traditions[7] in favor of a more cosmopolitan conception of "outsider democracy" that recognizes—and practices self-critically—antisubordination insights and imperatives. For this reason, some have described LatCrit as a "big tent" approach to critical outsider jurisprudence.

Democratic experiments do not aim or tend to create or "control" the artificial scarcities of professional recognition, intellectual legitimacy, or space in the pages of (elite) academic journals that are necessary specifically to imperial stratification of scholars and scholarship.[8] They aim, instead, to create diverse, programmatic, recurring opportunities for exchange and collaboration on multiple levels so that individual scholars can build alliances and networks as they develop their scholarly agendas and work, individually yet collectively, in the service of equal justice. As a democratic experiment, LatCrit aims self-consciously to commingle newcomers and veterans as knowledge-producing, community-building, and institution-sustaining actors. With this viewpoint, we encourage not only the immediate or short-term creation of elegant or incisive texts by today's "best and brightest" scholars but also an equal emphasis on enabling "junior" scholars to develop their talents, skills, and networks in the ongoing cultivation of a knowledge-producing discourse. This dual emphasis on individual and collective advancement shows how knowledge production is a multifaceted, many-splendored thing.

The democratic (or "big tent") approach therefore positively embraces difference and diversity across multiple categories, including empirical and technocratic definitions of "scholarship" as a form of knowledge production. While looking for substance and social relevance, democracy resists imposing fixed or universalized "standards" for scholarly production in the name of "quality" that, in fact, simply or mostly reflect and reinforce imperial projections of a false meritocracy. Indeed, this linkage of democratic practices with oppositional stances calls for deep, continual, and proactive critical reassessments of "quality" as constructed in a structurally racist, sexist, and homophobic culture.[9]

Additionally, and in keeping with the LatCrit commitment to anti-subordination goals and democratic practices, veteran (and sometimes more established) LatCrit scholars agreed, on principle and early on, to yield program slots in the conferences, as well as essay space in the accompanying written symposia, in order to ensure that junior or developing scholars were featured both in the live events and in the published works memorializing them. We similarly aimed to limit the substantive participation of each individual to a single slot or presentation in the formal program schedule. These and similar LatCrit choices were designed to check any tendency toward elitism—or the creation of a star system—within our projects and community. This emphasis on programmatic opportunities for junior scholars to develop and mature *critically* represents an oppositional or "dissenting" LatCrit stance within the still mostly imperial structures and biases of the U.S. legal academy.[10]

This collective decision of "senior" scholars to yield space and voice within LatCrit conferences and symposia to accommodate developing scholars also reflects the commitment to intergenerational community-building; it represents the aim of establishing a self-sustaining democratic structure for the incubation of antisubordination knowledge and action. This practice has cultivated layers and cohorts of scholars with diverse intellectual agendas and personal backgrounds who are commonly committed to the promotion of equal justice in symbolic and material terms. This cultivation of understanding and solidarity helps to create a sturdy support structure for the production of scholarship not only throughout the academic year but also, perhaps, throughout a lifetime and through changing life circumstances in ways that transcend the isolated dots of time oftentimes represented by conferences and other similar academic events.

To the undiscerning eye, the LatCrit experiment—and other democratic efforts—may appear to be "messy" when compared to the relatively familiar or controlled practices of the traditional models of knowledge production. Rather, democratic unruliness is a reflection of the open intellectual society that the LatCrit community has sought to bring into existence and cultivate. To us, the apparent messiness of outsider democracy is a sign of vitality and vigor rather than a defect to be quashed. This apparent unruliness is a reflection of the fact that the democratic model tends to generate a more substantively diverse body of discourse even though—or perhaps because—the programmatic structures employed tend to be more tailored to fostering the personal and intellectual engagement of difference. This multidimensional diversity should not be mistaken for inadvertent disarray.

On the contrary, this proactive engagement of difference in multiple ways across multiple axes of identification produces not only knowledge but also solidarity in the service of equal justice action. Our multiple forms and levels of engagement tend to cultivate the openness, understanding, and motivation necessary for antisubordination collaboration across multiple categories of identity—including across intra-"Latina/o/x" axes of difference; this attention to difference and diversity helps to set the stage for critical coalitions that stand on shared and enduring principles rather than temporarily converging interests. In our experience, the act and process of collaboration over time deepens levels of mutual understanding and trust that progressively enable greater intellectual and discursive risks, which oftentimes yield important epiphanies and create bonds of mutual respect and engagement. A sense of community enriches any kind of knowledge-production activity, both in the short and the long terms. Over time, collaboration incubates the social and intellectual conditions for organized academic activism in personal as well as in programmatic terms.

My impression of LatCrit . . . was that it, as an organization and as a movement, embraced the utopian vision of solidarity and connection across, through, and because of difference that I had grown up in the shadow of. People talked openly of their critical commitments. They believed in liberation. They questioned foundational givens of privilege whether it was race, gender, sexuality, nationality, disability, class, or educational privilege. People were, of course, flawed. And conversations were, as always in such circumstances, difficult. But the aspirational air in the room was unparalleled. Not only was it OK to be a progressive and critical scholar. This was a place where critique was centered. And it included everyone from everywhere. Islamic feminists in hijabs laughed over coffee with black lesbian feminists. Chicano queer scholars made common cause with their Cubano brothers and sisters from Miami. Postcoloniality became a vibrant and urgent concern with indigenous people and faculty from the global south in the room. Filipinas and Mexicans bonded in Spanish over shared challenges in academia. And we said aloud what everyone else pretended was false. The ranking system is about class privilege and race privilege. Star systems reproduce hierarchies of marginalization and inequality. And as a matter of aesthetics, the community embraced mestizo consciousness in theory and in praxis. Hybridity was centered. Complexity was embraced. And, even when there were challenges, there was really no place in the academy quite like it.

—Saru Matambanadzo[11]

LatCrit's organized, intergenerational, forward-looking approach to programs and community is seen in the steady, proactive inclusion of students in LatCrit conferences and projects. From the start, students from the United States and Global South have been welcomed—and sometimes featured—as participants like any other. In addition, as we elaborate below, we have built a fragile mini-pipeline from student to scholar consisting of several mutually reinforcing projects.

The establishment of the Junior Faculty Development Workshop (FDW), held for the first time in Cleveland during LatCrit VIII in 2003 and annually ever since, is one example—a venue and resource to support the efforts of rising critical generations of legal scholars and teachers in democratic and diverse terms. Initially held at the outset of each LatCrit annual conference, the FDW since 2012 found a home in even-numbered years connected to, and cosponsored by, the similarly biennial Society of American Law Teachers (SALT) teaching conference. This annual project, in partnership with SALT, covers key topics like pedagogy and publications, as well as the norms and politics of working in educational institutions, to ensure long-term advancement and success. This process helps to diversify the legal academy and to build critical networks.

I found the FDW and the rest of the SALT conference a welcoming and inspiring space. The camaraderie I encountered encouraged me, a very shy and reserved person, to engage and offer my perspective as one of the youngest (if not the youngest) and newest members of LatCrit, and someone with multiple subordinating identities. It also felt oddly familiar; in that space, I got to witness law professors grappling with the same questions that I had: how do we balance legal theory with practice while ensuring legal scholarship is grounded in and informed by the perspectives of subordinated communities? The LatCrit community continues to be a space for me to grow, a space that values and even seeks my contributions. In the years since my first FDW, I was honored as a LatCrit Student Scholar for my article on the institutionalized racism and homophobia in U.S. asylum law. . . . In short, LatCrit has treated me as a valuable asset. This is how social justice, non-profit organizations should work: by supporting and cultivating marginalized people as a way to challenge the dominant norms and practices of subordination.

—Zsea Bowmani[12]

Although the FDW is focused on new law teachers, we also sponsor recurring mentoring programs for junior and prospective scholars at other stages of their development. For example, as imagined and originally implemented by LatCrit organizers Angela Harris, Francisco Valdes, Margaret Montoya, and Sumi Cho, the LatCrit Student Scholar Program (SSP) seeks to diversify the legal academy with activist scholars from historically underrepresented communities. As in past years, selected participants in the 2019 SSP program were reimbursed for their travel to the 2019 LatCrit biennial conference, encouraged to present their papers there, invited to contribute to the LatCrit symposium issue for that conference, and introduced to a volunteer faculty mentor to assist their professional development. Since LatCrit awarded its first cohort of "Student Scholars" in 2003, the SSP has helped more than a dozen awardees obtain teaching positions at law schools and other departments in the United States and Canada.[13] Today, alumni of this program, like Marc-Tizoc González, continue to administer it.

As a set, these programmatic efforts constitute a fragile pipeline into teaching and research positions, which aims to support individuals throughout an entire career. This emphasis on democracy, pipeline, and succession, though carried out in varied ways, over time yields a common attention to both continuity and progression in the programmatic production of diverse scholars as well as diverse scholarship. This community-building helps to create the "big tent"—the structural, social, and intellectual conditions of knowledge production for diversely situated individual scholars with a common interest in promoting anti-subordination consciousness and action.

Put simply, I would not be a tenured law professor without LatCrit's inspirational body of scholarship, opportunities to workshop early drafts, and formal and informal mentorship. In moments of self-doubt and questioning whether I belong in the academy—as a woman of color from an underclass background, who had once dropped out of junior high school, who had been homeless as a child, and who is a single mother—the LatCrit intellectual and social community has been there to remind me that my outsiderness actually makes me effective in the classroom, on the pages of law review articles, and on the ground advocating for social justice. LatCrit has opened my mind and opened doors for me. I am confident they will continue to do so for future generations of outsider jurisprudence and praxis scholars and teachers.
—Jasmine Gonzalez Rose[14]

Even as this personal yet programmatic approach makes space for new voices and cultivates succession, LatCrit as a community also honors its

FIGURE 4.1. Critical Pioneer Award Ceremony, LatCrit XXI, Orlando, Florida

"elders." Reflecting and celebrating this range of voices are the community awards established in 2017: respectively, the Angela Harris Junior Scholar Award and the Critical Pioneer Award, the latter renamed in 2019 as the Francisco Valdes Critical Pioneer Award. At the same time, we established the Margaret Montoya Writing Workshop to support junior scholars, which has gathered at LatCrit's Campo Sano ("Wellness Camp") annually since then.[15] Additionally, at each biennial conference we feature the Jerome McCristal Culp, Jr., Memorial Lecture to remember, honor, and further Jerome's work as a critical pioneer.

This combination of proactive institution-building and community-building within LatCrit has taken the "safe space" concept beyond the momentary fragments of time and exchange created through a single, small, or closed gathering. By expanding programs that bring *us* together, we effectively expand the safe "space" into a safe "zone" that ranges across multiple activities throughout the year. The move from "space" to "zone" thus signifies, and helps to create, a broader and deeper

democratized location for diverse knowledge-production activities—
both individuated and collective—throughout the entire span of
each year, and through and across the years and generations, on self-
governing terms.

Creating a Base: The Pivotal Role of LatCrit Conferences in Theory, Community, and Praxis

LatCrit theory self-consciously endeavors both the creation of scholarship through community and the creation
of community through scholarship. The idea of, and need
for, regularized meetings accordingly have been integral to
the constitution of LatCrit theory, and to the production of
a LatCrit body of legal literature generated in connected,
rather than atomized, conditions.

—Francisco Valdes[16]

FIGURE 4.2. Jerome McCristal Culp, Jr., Memorial Lecture, LatCrit XXI, Orlando,
Florida

The five sets of scholarly contributions detailed in chapter 3—whose topics have also occupied the attention of antisubordination scholars of many stripes—accumulated in the form of individual published texts as well as collective or programmatic actions. To map key aspects of substantive contributions since LatCrit's inception in 1995, the following brief account of conference program themes outlines how LatCrit scholars have pursued those five lines of intellectual inquiry institutionally—that is, in collective, coalitional terms as community expressions of shared OutCrit values and commitments. This conceptual and theoretical mapping as background reveals that each annual (and now biennial) conference, and each conference theme, represented a building block in consistent programmatic efforts to construct a sturdy antisubordination jurisprudence in the form of LatCrit theory, community, and praxis.

In the earliest years, the LatCrit conferences were characterized by a proactive planning committee that sought affirmatively to apply the lessons of our precursors to and within this new jurisprudential experiment. To a significant extent, during those early years, LatCrit conference themes focused on the issues that then were deemed most controversial within Critical Race Theory and/or feminist legal scholarship, including issues of sameness/difference in social, cultural, or knowledge-production contexts.[17] Compared to most existing critical or outsider venues, these conferences featured very diverse programs, were open to all participants, and emphasized programmatic continuity. Based on accumulating experience and knowledge, LatCrit programs always try to gather the diversities necessary for difference to produce and expand knowledge.

As a result, during the early years we forged specific programmatic techniques, such as "rotating centers" and "streams of programming" discussed above, designed to build on prior and ongoing critical experiments—but on more democratic terms. And, as with the other "democratic" experiments, the original LatCrit annual conference has since expanded into a "portfolio" of collaborative initiatives designed

COMMUNITY AND METHOD | 51

to broaden and deepen this work in self-sustaining terms: although the annual/biennial conferences and related symposia were the original programmatic expression of this enterprise, our tripartite focus on theory, community, and praxis soon yielded a portfolio of multiyear projects designed to incubate theory *and* inform action. This approach amounted to long-term community organizing across many kinds of differences through coalitional academic activism.

As reflected in the conference themes of the first five LatCrit conferences, the first half of LatCrit's first decade shows how we proceeded programmatically in pursuit of the functions and guideposts described in chapter 2. The first annual conference, in San Diego, focused on Latina/o/x pan-ethnicity and questioned intra-Latina/o/x sameness and difference to help dislodge essentialized notions of this social group, as well as to explore the similarities and differences that might affect intragroup coalitions and communities. The next year, in San Antonio's LatCrit II conference, we followed up with a direct focus on difference, coalition, and community, which expanded the focus of our inquiry from intra to both intra- and intergroup contexts. Having "rotated the center" from intra- to intergroup issues in the first two years, we "streamed" this basic focus during the following two years. At LatCrit III in Miami, we thematized the notion of "comparative Latinas/os/x" to build on the first two years of inquiry regarding intra- and intergroup issues, while at LatCrit IV in Lake Tahoe, we built on this effort by focusing specifically on "marginal intersections." Both of these themes aimed to center categories—whether based on race, ethnicity, nationality, religion, sexuality, gender, or other typically marginalized aspects of identity—that oftentimes are erased in law or in Latina/o/x studies. Finally, we concluded the first half of the first decade, in Breckenridge, Colorado, by turning our collective programmatic attention at LatCrit V to the relationship of class identity to other forms of identity. Year by year, then, collectively we endeavored to produce a more intersectional, co-synthetic, interconnective, and multidimensional understanding of injustice.

FIGURE 4.3.LatCrit IX, Malvern, Pennsylvania

Subsequently, the conference themes during the second half of the first decade endeavored to build on the identity-focused explorations of those first five years. In Gainesville, Florida, the LatCrit VI conference theme turned our attention squarely to Global South-North issues and interconnections, while the next year, at LatCrit VII in Portland, Oregon, we focused on social movements as a category of study to better understand our own enterprise. The following year, the LatCrit VIII conference in Cleveland centered the "city" to underscore the material settings that house and frame so many within the populations we seek to help. Reflecting the zeitgeist of these times, we thematized "Kulturkampf," or cultural warfare, in the Philadelphia suburb of Malvern the subsequent year, thus investigating the larger societal dynamic prevailing during our own formative years.[18] Finally, at LatCrit X in San Juan, Puerto Rico, we returned to the relationship among material hierarchies, identity politics, and legal injustice. Whether viewed as a progression of ten steps, or as two sets of five steps each, the conference themes of LatCrit's first decade illustrated how this community endeavored programmatically to apply the lessons learned from prior jurisprudential experiments, as well as to advance antisubordination knowledge and action with and through LatCrit theory and praxis.

We began LatCrit's second decade with a continued focus on material justice in both local and global levels, convening for LatCrit XI in Las Vegas as a microcosm of globalized neoliberalism and its damage across multiple sectors of humanity. In Miami for LatCrit XII, we shifted focus, as we periodically do, to the nuts and bolts of our social roles and responsibilities as legal knowledge producers in a highly legalistic society. The following two years, at LatCrit XIII and XIV in Seattle and Washington, D.C., respectively, we kept our attention on democracy as concept and practice, examining both the operation of formal democracy today as well as the relationship of critical outsider theory and praxis to

FIGURE 4.4. LatCrit X, San Juan, Puerto Rico

FIGURE 4.5. LatCrit XV, Denver, Colorado

contemporary policy-making. At LatCrit XV in Denver the next year, we returned to the relationship of class to color, and vice versa, in the context of the "Great Bush Recession" starting in late 2008. When we convened in San Diego for our sixteenth annual conference in 2011, we again expanded our focus toward the theories, histories, and futures of global justice. Over the years, this series of programs promoted social identity as an antisubordination tool for critical knowledge and organized, coalitional action.

Thereafter, LatCrit switched to a biennial conference model in order to "open" space in the annual schedule of academic gatherings and to redirect resources to other recurrent projects. In this shift, the development of LatCrit theory, community, and praxis would continue unabated during the time between biennial conferences through a variety of projects such as the Study Space Seminar (SSS) and the South-North Exchange on Theory, Law, and Culture (SNX). Similarly, the Student Scholar Program and FDW, with their goal of mentoring prospective

Figures 4.6 and 4.7. LatCrit XVI, San Diego, California

faculty and junior scholars, continued their annual sessions to maintain our pipeline. All are run by overlapping small groups of volunteers.

Always mindful of the zeitgeist in which we live and labor, the first LatCrit biennial conference, held in 2013 in Chicago, focused on organizing generational transitions and building cross-sector, cross-constituency movements. At the twentieth-anniversary LatCrit biennial conference, held in Southern California in 2015, we launched a multiyear intervention into constitutional law's potential utility to outgroups pursuing antisubordination ends to stem the tides of retrenchment and regression. In the wake of the stunning 2016 U.S. presidential election, LatCrit's subsequent biennial conference, in 2017 in Orlando, asked and debated as a community "what's next" for outsider jurisprudence and progressive formations. Responding to the anti-equality onslaughts of this historical moment, LatCrit's most recent biennial conference, held in 2019 in Atlanta, offered a program and venue to strategize cooperative resistance of the dispossessed majority specifically to the neofascist turn in U.S. politics.

As this brief outline indicates, and the appendices affirm, LatCrit programs and projects take place across many different kinds of physical locations—cities, towns, hotels, universities, and conference centers. Sometimes, we even manage to get a bit of "spa-like splendor."[19] Most times, we don't. For instance, over the years LatCrit conferences have ranged from San Diego, California's La Jolla area, where the first annual conference convened, to Malvern, a nondescript suburb of Philadelphia, to a Chicago airport hotel, to a downtown Atlanta law school, and to Miami Beach and San Juan hotels. Wherever we might convene, we aim to tackle contentious real-world issues such as immigration, violence, and exploitation, as well as issues within academia such as diversity, pedagogy, and social justice.[20]

Whether focused on identity, community, nation-states, the academy, or the globe, our programmatic initiatives, particularly the annual and now biennial conferences, continue to provide platforms for individual scholars to exchange ideas, build understanding, envision social justice, and incubate academic activism in personal and programmatic terms. As both substance and method, these conferences and themes exemplify original and continuing LatCrit commitments to theory, community, and praxis in the pursuit of a postsubordination society. They are collective actions to organize ourselves autonomously within and beyond the U.S. legal academy. Despite their limitations, these conferences provide a programmatic context for the development of "personal collective praxis" as a conscious method of critical outsider jurisprudence in the service of equal justice progress.

Over time, these conferences (and similar programmatic projects outlined in the appendices) help to connect individual scholars based in dispersed locations or institutions, and belonging to different generations or communities, to congregate for action in principled and accountable terms. In and through these recurrent events we not only expand and deepen our personal and collective knowledge—both during our time together as well as through the resulting publications and projects—but also build for the longer term the relations of kinship and trust that are a prerequisite to antisubordination solidarity. These programmatic venues over time help to nurture the academic activism for which the LatCrit community has become known since 1995.

Because to the future we must look today, as always, with hope and courage. To that end, I would like to share some of the excellent ideas that I heard from the community at the [2017 Orlando] LatCrit Conference and beyond. First and foremost, I heard a resounding recognition of the value of the LatCrit Conferences themselves. The community left absolutely no doubt in my mind that it wishes to continue to meet in the big tent format that the LatCrit Conferences provide. . . . I encourage you all to reach out to the members of the Board of Directors and let us know how you can help in planning and organizing conferences in the future.

—Jorge Roig[21]

Navigating the Challenges of Academic Activism:
Resistance, Opportunity, Conflict[22]

> [LatCrit] activities and programs are designed to develop in-
> novative approaches to the production of knowledge from
> within the legal academy of the U.S., as well as to contest the
> entrenchment of interlocking hierarchies within the pro-
> fessoriate that are inconsistent with our antisubordination
> aspirations. . . . [We seek to construct] an enduring, alterna-
> tive counter-tradition to the ways and means of mainstream
> imperialism. This counter-tradition, focused on antisub-
> ordination academic activism, is based on the critical and
> self-critical application of OutCrit legal studies not only to
> society at large, not only to academia as a whole, but also to
> ourselves and all that we undertake.
> —Francisco Valdes[23]

As outlined throughout this Primer, critical outsider scholars have long
grappled over questions of coalition-building, community-building, and
institution-building in/as resistance to systemic injustice. Oftentimes,
if not always, these kinds of efforts require a commitment to collective
action even—perhaps especially—when individual will and incentives
tend toward a different direction. Academic activism as a collective
action of resistance to collectivized injustice is powerful precisely for
this reason: because individuals agree to act as a group.

However, group action is impracticable, sometimes impossible, un-
less individuals over time are willing to defer to each other at different times in ways always anchored to principles and methods that, by
mutual agreement, form the common bond of substantive solidarity.
Academic activism thus requires, at a minimum: (1) articulated common principles to serve as a substantive anchor for group action, and
against which group or individual actions may be measured; (2) practices to perform the common principles, both internally and externally,

in ethical and efficient ways; (3) long-term commitments to the coalitional project to foster trust and ensure continuity in the principles and practices of the group; and (4) specific practices to promote and manage group diversities and potential divergences. While other elements may be equally necessary, these four elements have proven key to LatCrit efforts to engage the issues and concerns underlying sameness/difference dilemmas in the praxis of academic activism—as our uses of rotating centers, shifting bottoms, and streams of programming illustrate.

These programmatic and substantive emphases on organized academic activism lend themselves to the broader project of making multiply diverse "Latinas/os/x" not only a relevant but also a positive force on the inter/national stages of politics and policy. For these reasons, the methods and lessons of the LatCrit community in democratic knowledge production and legal academic activism can serve as a microcosm of the opportunities and possibilities, as well as the difficulties, presented by the emergence of "Latinas/os/x" as a force to be reckoned with in (North) American society (and beyond). While LatCrits recognize that no approach is perfect, we hope our exertions offer helpful lessons to the coming generations(s) of scholars who will continue to work around this country and the globe on connecting academic knowledge production to academic social activism toward the goal of a postsubordination society.

Thus, organizing academic activism and/as knowledge production has been and remains an ongoing challenge within and outside the academy, as the afterword to this Primer makes even more clear. The same pressures that discourage student activism and incentivize students to act individually rather than collectively while disconnected from larger community and social campaigns also stifle academic activism among faculty. The same reward system that channels students into conformity also suppresses faculty activism, both within the academy and as connected to broader systemic struggles. The outcomes for students and faculty are intertwined. The system really does try to make resistance futile.

Nonetheless, through the decades, we look for cracks of opportunity. We organize in full sight using the system's tools—and our privileges—critically and creatively to resist the system itself. We use what we know about the system in order to think outside of its boxes and limits. We continue to build community and organize ourselves for the purpose of academic activism because, as we noted in the preface, we recognize that if we do not advocate and agitate for systemic change within the academy, then nobody will. To do so, we engage in long-term collective planning and follow-ups, but we also act opportunistically—when and where we can—so long as it is consistent with our shared values and commitments, as outlined in chapter 2. Individually and programmatically, we aim to be pragmatic *and* principled.

This work inevitably entails conflict as well as collaboration. Like all human groups, we've had periodic squabbles, some of them very serious. Like all self-aware human groups, we've also had principled conflicts over ideas or institutions, including, for instance, religion, which erupted in the midst of conference proceedings in San Antonio at LatCrit II. As is our practice, we stopped the planned proceedings, organized the chairs into a big circle around the room, and began an unplanned, sometimes heated, conversation.[24] Everyone learned from that experience and similar ones.[25] We grew together, and internal critique remains ongoing within LatCrit venues. We understand that conflict itself has to be engaged as community-building.

At LatCrit II, I experienced a LatCrit "moment." . . . We were in a room at St. Mary's University at the Center for Legal and Social Justice, a converted convent, that looked out onto a religious mural, a work by Brother Cletus of the Virgin of Guadalupe. Nancy Ota spoke out about how uncomfortable the place made her due to the religious iconography and, of course, the Catholic Church's role in oppressing sexual minorities. What happened next made me love LatCrit all the more. A discussion about sexual and race identity and the Catholic Church broke out. . . . I remember thinking how unique the conference was: these were people

speaking the truth about their experiences as sexual and racial minorities. Emotions were very raw, but the conversation proceeded as the session evolved into a very different conversation than the one that was advertised. The conversation was real, sincere, and genuine. I was amazed that [attendees] felt that the space was safe enough to carry out this type of conversation. It was difficult and tense, but thought provoking also.
—Roberto Corrada[26]

Community-building: From Individuals to Institutions and Coalitions

In this [LatCrit] organization, this movement, I have grown. I have found a place to be comfortable in my discomfort, among others who are similarly situated. I have found comrades and friends to laugh with, colleagues to share work with, and a commitment to serving the legal academy by supporting scholars of color and the critical and progressive members of the legal academy.
—Saru Matambanadzo[27]

LatCrit's focus on praxis,[28] or the performance of theory in and through multifold LatCrit projects, reflects another early priority: the commitment to building a critical community—a priority that also reflects the influence of LatCrit's precursors on our earliest efforts.[29] This emphasis, moreover, recognizes our humanity as integral to our work and aims to situate our efforts in the context of human conditions as we know them. But this aspect of the LatCrit enterprise did not track essentialized notions of sameness or similarity as the template for the community we imagined. Instead, community-building as LatCrit praxis called for a principled application of the functions, guideposts, postulates, and related standards detailed in chapter 2 to ourselves, to help us ensure operational fidelity to theoretical commitments. Thus, from the onset, community-building as LatCrit praxis was anchored to substantive commitments and to their self-critical application in the institutional context of the community projects we have undertaken.

As mentioned above, LatCrit's portfolio of projects was designed, assembled, and maintained as mutually reinforcing activities or venues that build on the "safe space" concept of our jurisprudential ancestors. Together, LatCrit programs and publications create a year-round and year-to-year safe zone for the incubation and dissemination of OutCrit legal studies. This priority attends to the need of outsider academics not only for formal success but also for diverse sites of self-critical and supportive gatherings that can help nourish us as critical scholars *and* as human beings. Our ongoing events are timed and organized to create ongoing opportunities for interested individuals who are generally like-minded to gather around substantive themes for the exchange of bottom-up ideas, the production of critical knowledge, and the cultivation of action networks. Typically, as this Primer's appendices show, these programmatic efforts are (partially) captured in the publications associated with most LatCrit programs since 1995.

The importance of community-building to the production of critical outsider jurisprudence cannot be overemphasized given the ambient dangers that confronted (and still confront, perhaps even more so) any progressive or critical undertaking in the United States and elsewhere. Two ambient dangers have been most salient. The first is the anticritical bent of the U.S. legal academy, which during the 1980s and 1990s engineered the "death" of critical legal studies and the banishment of "crits" from law faculties throughout the country; the second was the anti-identitarian backlash of the culture wars, which insisted on formal blindness to traditionally vexed identity categories such as race, gender, ethnicity, and class.[30] Under these circumstances, the safest and surest way to "succeed" as a legal scholar in the United States during the 1990s, and thereby gain institutional rewards, was to avoid guilt by association with "crits" and, more specifically, with critical projects of color. The existence of a self-identified "community" of LatCrit scholars, therefore, was and continues to be a collective act of defiance against the political juggernaut that demands conformity to dominant tradition and denies the daily violence of the status quo.[31]

Given the background and pressures outlined immediately above, four key and early features of LatCrit community-building stand out. The first is our decision to root community-building in mutual critical commitments, which form the normative baseline for this community and, ultimately, for all critical coalitions.[32] The second is our decision to incorporate (as Latina and Latino Critical Legal Theory, Inc., a Florida nonprofit corporation) and institutionalize our collective efforts in order to foster community-building based on this shared normative baseline and facilitate multiple opportunities for collective personal praxis in the form of the LatCrit portfolio of projects. The third key feature is our insistence on securing the conditions of independence, in substantive and in material terms, to clear the way for the ethical practice of our theoretical commitments. Finally, this emphasis on community-building also has prompted us to ensure that all our conferences and gatherings strive to foster the varied sorts of informal personal interactions that help to produce the human solidarity necessary to withstand the pressures of the day and to overcome the limitations of our individual and collective capacities. This emphasis also reflects CRT's influence on LatCrit's designs: during the CRT workshops, many participants, including the junior scholars that later became LatCrit pioneers, noticed that the informal, post-program conversations oftentimes took insights discussed during the day to deeper, exciting levels. We noticed that those conversations—oftentimes lasting until the wee hours of the next morning—forged not only theoretical refinements but also human relationships of understanding and solidarity. In a world that oscillates from hostility to indifference when it comes to critical theory and antisubordination praxis, this sense of scholarly solidarity was important glue. Over the years, the LatCrit Community Hospitality Suite, held at our various academic events throughout each year and often during the annual meeting of the Association of American Law Schools (AALS), has served this purpose directly.

The LatCrit Hospitality Suite is a living appendage to scholarship: so many ideas have been born there, so many ideas have been expanded and extended there.

—Roberto Corrada[33]

Today, this emphasis on community-building continues to guide our efforts and practices in all that we (might) do.[34] Reflecting our substantive concerns, as we will detail in chapter 6, in recent years the Global South has become more and more salient in our community-building, coalition-building, and institution-building efforts. Yet, at the same time, we have continued and intensified our efforts to operate varied collective initiatives that help to create and sustain safe spaces *and* zones within the U.S. legal academy. As with the substantive or intellectual

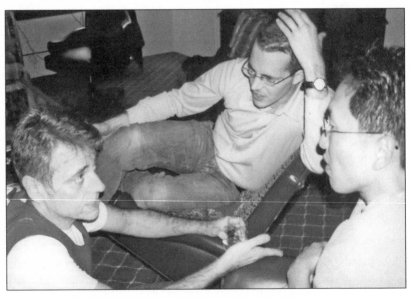

FIGURE 4.8. LatCrit IX, Malvern, Pennsylvania

evolution of our programs and projects, the varied levels of community-building in our personal collective praxis continue to expand and take new forms based on the ongoing, self-critical evaluation of experience from year to year.

This continuing effort is best exemplified by the thousand-day self-study and strategic planning process that the LatCrit community concluded in 2010 and by the substantive and institutional priorities generated democratically through that process. Those priorities reflect a considered analysis of the changing circumstances both within LatCrit/OutCrit ranks, as well as across the legal academy and, more broadly, the United States and the globe. These new priorities in some ways consolidate our gains thus far to reflect a renewed commitment to early or original goals, while others break new ground literally.[35] In each instance, however, these priorities, and our ongoing work, continue to be anchored in the original guideposts, functions, postulates, and hallmarks that provided early foundations for the old and new communal directions we have pursued since LatCrit's inception. While adapting to changing circumstances both internally and externally, LatCrit and allied scholars continue to have a clear sense of a postsubordination mission going forward, anchored as always to the values, principles, and practices that we have shared for more than two decades of intellectual and institutional work.

Perhaps LatCrit's deepest collaboration with another institution has been its ongoing affiliation with the Society of American Law Teachers. Progressive law professors organized SALT in 1973, as they recognized the need to impact public policy while also responding to the teaching opportunities created by the increasing numbers of nontraditional students—young people of color, women, Vietnam veterans, gays and lesbians, and those from low-income families—with innovative law school curricula and pedagogy.[36] Facing internal challenges about its lack of racial and gender diversity, particularly in its leadership, SALT eventually underwent an infusion of leadership from the LatCrit community, and increasing collaboration ensued.[37] Although LatCrit, unlike

SALT, collects no membership fees and seeks community members from related disciplines and from the Global South, both organizations go about their nontraditional business by prioritizing, in systematized ways, intergenerational community-building through serious institution-building.

Over the years, LatCrit has collaborated with SALT to draft and submit antibias amicus briefs in cutting-edge controversies and performed other pro bono legal/scholarly work on behalf of poor and marginalized communities. Most significantly, to ensure a pipeline for law teachers from subordinated groups, LatCrit and SALT collaborated to host the annual FDW. Initially, the FDW met immediately before the LatCrit annual conference and was organized by the same conference planning committee. Eventually, LatCrit and SALT made the mutual decision (in light of scarcity of time and other resources) to alternate their fall conferences, with the FDW to take place annually at both alternating conferences starting in 2012. Program planning has also become more interorganizational. These collaborations illustrate the kind of daily, coalitional, programmatic work that outsider democracy facilitates, and they have helped to nurture the kind of sisterly organizational relationship that allows for the deep levels of cooperation that our alternating conferences exemplify.

LatCrit's other institutional affiliations include a growing number of law schools that have contributed toward its annual/biennial conference, as indicated in each program schedule. In addition, these affiliations have focused on specific initiatives or projects, including: the University of California, Berkeley law school and other law schools that have supported LatCrit's Student Scholar Program; the Universidad InterAmericana de Puerto Rico, Facultad de Derecho (UIAPR), the University of Pittsburgh School of Law, and other law schools that have supported the SNX; the University of Baltimore School of Law and other law schools that have supported the Critical Global Classroom (CGC); and the University of Miami School of Law that has supported LatCrit institutionally, as well as several startup projects, over the years.

LatCrit from its inception additionally has sought institutional collaborations through publication projects with Latina/o/x- and other subordinated-identity-related journals as well as more generalized law reviews. As detailed in the appendices, most events to date have been cosponsored by or otherwise affiliated with one or more law journals, which publish short edited pieces that provide substantive snapshots of the conference proceedings. This feature of the LatCrit enterprise seeks to support and build coalition with law reviews (especially those journals of color) while also creating collective projects and opportunities for all participants in LatCrit programs. This particular aspect of the LatCrit venture has been tailored to provide support and community to scholars and to journals while igniting the creation of a new field in legal literature. By producing a similarly diversified printed record of our gatherings and exchanges, this feature of LatCrit projects advances the antiessentialist analyses and antisubordination aims of this movement with respect to community and to theory. This type of ongoing publication project helps to create not only links between students and faculty but also a written record of our proceedings that enables a kind of permanent "virtual attendance" at our events. Over the years, collaboration with law reviews enables the cultivation of knowledge among student editors who can be the future agents of social and legal transformation. As the record shows, from the inception of LatCrit we made a firm commitment to the publication of the proceedings of the annual (now biennial) conferences and, later and as discussed below, of the smaller gatherings that take place regularly as part of our portfolio of projects.

Recognizing fully that law review symposia historically have been structured in various ways in light of different circumstances or objectives—and that sometimes they foster a "community of meaning" while other times they amount to a "re-inscription of hierarchy"[38]— LatCrit scholars opted decisively, also from the beginning, in favor of the former. From the outset, the specific symposium structure was designed consciously (if imperfectly) to promote democratic values of access and participation; to encourage experimentation with formats, bibliographic sources, multilinguality, and forms of expression; as well as to expand the dissemination of knowledge produced or presented during the conference programs or that was "inspired" by them.

In addition to publications centered around conference proceedings, the LatCrit record of publications includes law review symposia connected to programs, like the SNX, the International and Comparative Law Colloquium (ICC), and the Study Space Seminars,[39] as well as freestanding law review symposia distinct from those proceedings. These freestanding projects include an early joint publication by Berkeley's *California Law Review* (1997) and *La Raza Law Journal* (1998), branching out in various early but influential directions on *Latinidad* in the United States, followed in 2000 by a joint publication in the *Michigan Journal of Race and Law* and the *Michigan Journal of Law Reform* that focused specifically on introducing interdisciplinary scholarship and centering questions of culture, nation, and power in LatCrit discourse. The most recent freestanding publication was a collection of LatCrit pieces around the theme of seeking equal justice in law, education, and society, showcasing a number of relatively junior LatCrit scholars and published in 2015 by the *Chicago-Kent Law Review.*

Similarly, the LatCrit record of publications also includes a 2018 book published jointly by the ABA Section of International Law and Carolina Academic Press, titled *From Extraction to Emancipation: Development Reimagined*, that grew out of a Study Space in Guatemala. This project-based book offered an alternate vehicle for LatCrit knowledge production in the form of published and "peer-reviewed" trade books, as well as other kinds of books. Since then, in addition to this Primer, our most recent book projects include the textbook *Critical Justice: Systemic Advocacy in Law and Society* (discussed in chapter 6), which is intended for classroom users as well as for other readers.

Finally, LatCrit publications include the founding of, and collaboration with, CLAVE, a critical legal journal initially published jointly by LatCrit and the UIAPR. "Clave" (kla:ve) is the Spanish word for "key"— "un punto clave" is "a key point." Additionally, in Afro-Cuban and other styles of music, claves are the rhythmic keys that organize a composition. We adopted the name seeking to embrace its denotations and connotations in full. From inception, this project disrupted traditional U.S. scholarly norms, featuring works in the Spanish language that likewise seek to transcend the traditional boundaries of nation, discipline, and academic hierarchy. Since its founding in 2000, CLAVE has published works drawn from disciplines related to law, including cultural studies, American studies, history, sociology, and anthropology, to explore the ways in which the state, through law, furthers the production of national, gendered, and racialized subjects. But CLAVE also has explored the many modes of resistance to state power built on colonialism and imperialism throughout today's diasporas. This collaboration continues, even though CLAVE has become a strong and self-sustaining organization in recent years.

In each instance, these (and similar) institutional collaborations are based on a shared ethic of antisubordination solidarity. As practiced, this ethic enables individuals to construct communities that build institutions, which cultivate critical coalitions based on knowledge and its progressive production. It is the steady programmatic practice of this activist ethic that has animated the LatCrit experiment in theory and praxis to become and survive as a *democratic* academic community despite multiple differences and during the increasingly trying times in which we work.

5

LatCrit Praxis

Personal, Collective, and "Glocal"

Coalitional Praxis: Making It Programmatic

> LatCrit theory self-consciously recognizes that theory with-
> out praxis severely constrains the purpose and utility of the-
> ory; praxis is constitutional to LatCrit theory because social
> transformation is a key function of legal theory.
> —Francisco Valdes

From the beginning, LatCrit has aimed to fuse theory to action in order
to "combust personal and collective action out of critical theory."[1] Each
LatCrit conference and each project reflect and demand attention to
praxis-oriented goals; our programs use theory to design actions and
use the lessons of action to produce theory for further action, both traditional and nontraditional. In this scheme, action is rooted in theory
and theory emerges from action. In this mix, some LatCrit endeavors
are particularly directed to domestic and/or international lawmaking,
ranging from the U.S. federal appeals courts to the United Nations (UN).
Two praxis-oriented projects described below illustrate this synergistic
mix. Both display the cooperative, coalitional bent of LatCrit praxis.

LatCrit strives to inject critical theory and insights into adjudication
and its outputs, often through litigation seeking transformative ends,
but other times aiming for short-term, more immediate amelioration
of evident injustice. Amicus curiae briefs have been the most common
procedural and substantive vehicle for this LatCrit intervention. Most
significantly, LatCrit submitted an amicus curiae brief in the ultimately

successful struggle over Arizona's anti–ethnic studies statute deployed to prohibit the teaching in the Tucson school district of Mexican American Studies, a curriculum steeped in critical history.[2] With the aid of and collaboration with Seattle-based law firm K&L Gates LLP, LatCrit's brief fused constitutional arguments with critical history that framed the current struggle within the long history of efforts to obtain educational equality in Arizona, once a venue for schools formally and purposefully segregated to keep Mexican American children separate from whites. The anti–ethnic studies law aimed to ensure the teaching of a sanitized white version of history that keeps Mexican American children separated from their own histories of exclusion, separation, and loss, thereby precluding the critical thinking and organizing that could emerge from these studies. Another prominent example is the LatCrit amicus curiae brief, filed in partnership with the Society of American Law Teachers, urging a federal appeals court to constitutionally protect food-sharing with the homeless as expressive conduct and peaceable assembly.[3] In the coming months and years, LatCrit is particularly alert to opportunities to contribute toward Black Lives Matter and related struggles to resist police brutality and mass incarceration that have galvanized so many protests in addition to backlash in support of the "law and order" status quo.[4]

The efforts mentioned above used traditional legal means to inject critical knowledge into domestic legal decisions, but we have endeavored the same across borders. As an additional example of a praxis project, in this case one seeking global impact, in 2006 LatCrit obtained consultative status from the UN Economic and Social Council and has successfully sought and obtained accreditation renewals every five years since. In the form of an accredited nongovernmental organization (NGO), LatCrit pursues two interrelated and ongoing goals:

> (1) the interjection of critical and comparative analyses and arguments regarding identity subordination into current dialogues within international legal and political institutions; and

(2) the provision of experiential learning opportunities for students as authors and advocates of [such] analyses and arguments.[5]

In that role, LatCrit's NGO project has urged a number of antisubordination-oriented re-visionings of international law, such as proposing that "receiving governments must recognize, decriminalize, legitimize, legalize, and regulate the massive flows of low wage labor migration that take place throughout—and are indispensable to—the global economy."[6] And to maximize the potential of this organizational accreditation, we also routinely have shared (or "loaned") our UN credentials so that like-minded groups and persons can access UN venues or channels that otherwise are closed. Combining our personal and collective efforts with others through this NGO project exemplifies our open, coalitional approach to theory, community, and praxis.

Although we mention amicus community projects and the accredited NGO as two specific programmatic examples of LatCrit domestic and international praxis as open and coalitional, we also design and carry out all our projects similarly. As we noted in chapter 4, our conferences (and other events) are organized to cultivate an activist academic community committed to both knowledge and action. Indeed, our entire "portfolio of projects" has been developed as mutually reinforcing expressions of our abiding commitment to praxis, both in our workplaces and profession—the legal academy—and in society, both in the United States and abroad. Without praxis at the center, we realize theory becomes wooden, and action becomes irrelevant to justice. We organize everything we do as personal yet collective praxis because experience teaches that principled and accountable collaborations are the only chance we get to obtain equal justice.

But, crucially, this approach to personal collective praxis is focused on establishing *programmatic* initiatives capable of outliving their originators. One-time events or efforts may be best for some contexts, but usually not; as this account of organized academic activism underscores, long-term and collaborative efforts—programmatic initiatives—are usually required for even the tiniest of systemic changes. For this reason, LatCrit projects are designed and administered to be sustainable as well as self-sustainable. For this reason, LatCrit praxis is coalitional as well as programmatic.

Border Crossings: Global South Salience

> Although the earliest LatCrit/OutCrit work focused on issues within the US, lines of inquiry [since] have expanded and deepened this work toward increasingly globalized and localized contexts. This commitment to globalized contextualism aims to connect the legal and the social both at the micro/local level and at the macro/global level through OutCrit scholarship that conjoins the interrogation of legal, cultural, and material realities. For instance, this work strives to "bring home" international rights, to bridge "domestic" and "foreign" spheres of policy and action, to infuse comparative studies with a critical sensibility, and to foster a general appreciation and embrace of internationalism in the development of critical legal scholarship.
> —Francisco Valdes[7]

From its earliest years, LatCrit and allied scholars experimented with long-term programmatic initiatives with a global emphasis, situated in venues outside the mainland United States—like the International and Comparative Law Colloquium and the Critical Global Classroom—to give institutional, collective expression toward internationalism and comparativism in/as LatCrit theory and praxis. The ICC helped U.S.-based LatCrit scholars engage scholars from other regions on issues of common interest to social justice advocates, as appendix C details. The CGC summer program, often held in conjunction with the ICC, in turn aimed to provide critical, progressive students—particularly those from schools devoid of offerings steeped in criticality—better access (indeed, a lifeline) to outsider jurisprudence and to each other.[8] Since the mid-1990s, LatCrit international projects have emerged, coalesced, adapted, and expanded into several programmatic initiatives.

In the 2000s, we initiated two more distinctive programmatic global efforts: the South-North Exchange on Theory, Law, and Culture in partnership with the UIAPR, and the Study Space Seminar originally in partnership with Georgia State University College of Law. Each provides a different mechanism to help the LatCrit community develop mutually reinforcing, border-crossing programs. Both are designed to foster transnational *and* cross-disciplinary encounters, insights, and networks, and both have also included student participants.

The SNX, as its name denotes, has emphasized South-North framings and the cultivation of critical studies and networks particularly across the Americas and, more generally, with and within the Global South. In addition, as the name likewise denotes, this project is designed to be a conversational (and praxis) exchange not only across region or location but also across discipline and perspective—an exchange of theory, law, and culture in an ongoing examination of their interplay. The basic concept is to create a venue focused on South-North relations, and on issues that affect or constitute South-North polarities, to strengthen LatCrit theory, community, and praxis in hemispheric terms. As appendix D illustrates, since its initial program at the campus of the UIAPR School of Law in San Juan, Puerto Rico, in 2003, the annual and now biennial SNX has taken place at a variety of venues, primarily across the Global South Americas, to focus critical attention on various substantive themes ranging from issues of constitutional reform to the struggles of Indigenous people. Over time, this project aims to nurture not only a discourse but also a network of global critical scholars able to multiply our knowledge-production work as equal justice praxis.

More recently, from 2007, the Study Space Seminar is another LatCrit programmatic innovation similarly designed to cultivate both community and knowledge across location, identity, and discipline. This project assembles a relatively small number of academics, students, and activists from both the Global South and Global North for a week or longer to attend an immersion workshop convened in rotating cities and regions around the world in order to study those locations as human habitats and as venues for antisubordination work.[9] Since 2007, the SSS has centered and visited Panama City, Panama (2007); Bogotá, Colombia (2008); Denver, Colorado, (2008); Medellín, Colombia (2009); Rio de Janeiro, Brazil (2010); Havana, Cuba (2013); and a variety of rural and urban locations in Guatemala (2015), with plans in additional venues to include Quito, Ecuador. This project aims to synthesize the formal study and experiential understanding of material realities in these locales and their systemic correlation to traditional identity-based ideologies deployed through race, gender, sexuality, and other troubled categories. As appendix E illustrates, in and through the SSS, participants are able to understand in both intellectual and physical terms how the construction of socioeconomic classes intersects with white supremacy, patriarchy, homophobia, and other identity-based neo/colonial ideologies across particular habitats. Over time, these rotating seminars effectively produce a map of varied locations with remarkably similar commonalities amid their many complexities and intricacies; they create a map of law, identity, and in/justice showing both specificities and commonalities as well as collectivizing resistance to these realities. Over time, this project, like and with the ICC, CGC, SNX, and other LatCrit projects, helps to cultivate a sense of activist academic community across multiple borders based on shared commitments to a postsubordination reality.[10]

This collective basket of LatCrit's internationalist/comparativist projects parallels LatCrit's programmatic efforts to establish a critical outsider counter-tradition within the United States based on democratic practices and antisubordination values through the annual/biennial conferences and other "domestic" programs in the LatCrit portfolio. These globally oriented projects and their related publications strive to create conducive intellectual conditions for the articulation of critical outsider jurisprudence in South-North legal frameworks. These and similar projects constitute a long-term proactive campaign to cultivate a diverse and coalitional academic micro-society without borders, a transnational community of critical networks committed to equal justice knowledge and action.

Expanding the scope of our U.S.-based programs, each of these projects aims to provide a cross-cultural "safe space" for the incubation specifically of diverse inter-American justice networks, studies, and actions. As a set, these global projects cumulatively aim to provide a transnational "zone" of safety where these diverse, transgenerational, antisubordination networks, discourses, and efforts can meet, grow, and strengthen. These efforts to conceive and initiate new fields of study and action aim to open lines of critical, cross-disciplinary inquiry adapted to the mapping and undoing of structural patterns of domination across the Americas and even beyond. These efforts to foment a kind of "hemispheric justice studies" have yielded multilateralized discourses, publications, networks, and projects designed to help North-centric scholars and scholarship learn from South-centric work and vice versa.[11] This type of sustained multilateral exchange aims to coalesce with social justice advocates across the Americas (and beyond) to catalyze and sustain positive social change within societies and across borders.[12] Organizing academic activism in the United States and beyond, as best as we can, is our way of contributing to these broader efforts.

LatCrit can be instrumental in suggesting and proposing ways to conceptualize differences and commonalties in designing an agenda to promote the recognition and enforcement of human rights in domestic and international fora. . . .

The indisputably suprasovereign nature of fundamental human rights offers LatCrit theory fertile ground on which to develop conceptions of law that will be of significance to the comunidad latina as well as to all other communities in our midst. For example, with sovereignty ceding to basic human rights principles, it follows logically that human rights norms can trump local law which derogates from such principles.

Considering current issues of interest and activism, the immigration rights discourse provides a significant forum in which to apply the theory [of the preeminence of international human rights principles] to practice.
—Berta Esperanza Hernández-Truyol[13]

Webs of Collaboration: LatCrit's Portfolio of Projects and Teams

[T]he LatCrit "portfolio of projects" constitutes the concrete forms of "collective personal praxis" that has become a LatCrit hallmark. . . .

. . . To meet the challenges that enable a critical transcending of difference and a mutual cultivation of critical communities and coalitions, we have consciously employed the annual conferences and the entire LatCrit Portfolio of Projects as a vehicle to make community-building, coalition-building and institution-building, integral to critical outsider jurisprudence.
—Berta Hernandez-Truyol, Angela P. Harris &
Francisco Valdes[14]

Finally, as this chapter and the previous ones help to illustrate, the LatCrit community has organized our programs and events around a "portfolio" of projects, both within and beyond the United States and its legal academy. Each community project is the product of a suggestion or of a recognized need. Each project is administered collaboratively by a team, usually three to five persons. Some project team members are academics while others are students, practitioners, or activists. Whenever possible, we include persons from outside of the United States or outside of law. Usually, team members are situated in different institutions and locations that are distant from each other.

Under these physical circumstances, collaboration is the key to any success. These projects and teams provide the infrastructure through

FIGURE 5.1. 2018 South-North Exchange, Antigua, Guatemala

which we can collaborate flexibly with each other across time and space to keep community efforts going. These diverse, dispersed teams work year-round by phone, email, Zoom, and the like; in addition, we gather in person periodically each year based on plans, resources, and circumstances. In cooperation and consultation with the LatCrit Board of Directors, this year-round teamwork produces both upcoming programs as well as long-term project development. This multiply-collaborative work sustains the "zones" of safety and the culture of democratic knowledge production sketched in chapter 4.

These projects—and their longer-term development—are designed to be as mutually reinforcing as possible. Sometimes we describe projects as falling into "baskets" based on their purposes so we can maximize their commonalities and compound their effects—perhaps the conjunction of the Faculty Development Workshop, the Student Scholar Program, and the annual/biennial LatCrit conferences exemplifies this point. "Synergy" is a word we use often, as is "collaboration."

6

Critical Pedagogy

Transforming Legal Education and Targeting Systemic Injustice

LatCrit in the Classroom: Identity, Power, and Knowledge

> Activist teaching, specifically what I'll call critical teach-
> ing, refers to a pedagogy that is sensitive to the fluidity of
> power relations, the constitutive nature of legal practices,
> and the synergies created by the metamorphoses of legal
> processes when distorted, altered, and reclaimed by Out-
> siders whose identities have multiple manifestations and
> expressions.
> —Margaret E. Montoya

Pedagogy has been a consistent emphasis in LatCrit conferences and symposia and in the classrooms of its community members.[1] One Lat-Crit member recounted that "[v]irtually every annual conference and the resulting symposia have dedicated a space for the exchange of criti-cal pedagogies and innovative teaching strategies. This concern with a critical approach to the teaching of law in the social realm has been informed by a concern with equality, difference, justice and a host of other critical commitments embraced by participating members."[2] As a result, critical legal pedagogy must make the connections between identity, power, law, and knowledge. It also must expose the absences, distortions, and limitations of formal legal training.

For instance, as with the general socio-legal invisibility of Latinas/os/x that helped prompt the emergence of LatCrit as a response, "La-tinas/os/x and the law" offerings in U.S. law schools were similarly invisible. This much was confirmed early on by an exhaustive LatCrit empirical study.[3] These findings (and personal experience) supported efforts by several community members to introduce into their law school curriculum new courses centering Latina/o/x issues; as a result, some law schools subsequently offered courses focused on LatCrit itself as a value-laden movement concerned with legal pedagogy as an instrument of equal justice.[4] This attention to curriculum, pedagogy, and justice reflects the need to transform the dominant system of legal education and its Socratic method–driven classrooms toward antisubordination means and ends. The objective of our attention to curricular development and critical pedagogy is to engage and embolden, rather than to stifle or silence, outsider students *and* teachers.

Critical pedagogy has been described as "an education theory and praxis that seeks by means of dialectical thinking and the constant exchange of ideas to liberate both teachers and students from the reified ideas that society has imposed upon us."[5] As developed within Critical Race Theory, critical pedagogy in education generally has basic perspectives, research methods, and teaching methods informed by at least five elements: (1) the centrality and intersectionality of race and racism; (2) the challenge to dominant ideology; (3) the commitment to social justice; (4) the importance of experiential knowledge; and (5) the use of interdisciplinary perspectives.[6] The aims of a critical pedagogy within LatCrit specifically, as articulated by LatCrit community members, include those above, as well as making five critical connections: (1) connecting the past to the present; (2) connecting the personal and the structural; (3) connecting the social and the legal; (4) connecting the particular and the general; and (5) connecting knowledge and practice.[7] As envisioned and practiced within LatCrit, faculty bring to the classroom a critical ethic of antisubordination analysis that pays attention both to the trees and to the forests of systemic injustice.[8] Using various means, critical pedagogy upends the subordinating norms and dynamics of the traditional classroom. As briefly highlighted below, these include attention to counterstorytelling through analytical narratives, silence as a hegemonic and counter-hegemonic tool, collaboration, community engagement, and the unearthing of hidden critical histories across the curriculum.

LatCrit community members invoke analytical narratives, particularly autobiography, in their scholarship, akin to CRT scholars, "as methods to challenge the ostensibly objective and neutral perspectives found in majority legal scholarship."[9] LatCrit scholars Angela Harris and Leslie Espinoza phrased this goal of narrative as trying to "'re-story' the past and 're-imagine' the future."[10] Relatedly, the practice of *testimonio* flows from critical self-reflection, in this case on the experience of confronting and surviving oppression, and then testifying to that struggle in the public sphere.[11] In the critical classroom, analytical narration is an antisubordination technique to connect the personal to the structural. Through what has been characterized as "counterstorytelling,"[12] students can encounter the experiences from those on the bottom of societal castes and learn a tool for analyzing and challenging the heretofore accepted stories of those in power.[13] These counterstories serve five pedagogical functions identified by LatCrit scholars: (1) They build community among those at the margins of society; (2) they challenge the perceived wisdom of those empowered at society's center; (3) they open new windows into the reality of outsiders by showing the possibilities beyond the ones they live and that they are not alone in their position; (4) they teach that, by combining elements from both the story and the current reality, one can construct another world richer than either the story or the reality alone; and (5) they provide a context to analyze, understand, and transform established belief systems,[14] particularly those otherwise fostered by traditional legal education.

LatCrit scholars additionally have shown how to use silence in the classroom as a pedagogical tool to challenge the communication style of dominant groups that privileges insiders and marginalizes the rest. Specifically, LatCrit and other progressive scholars of color use silence counter-hegemonically in the classroom and beyond: "[W]e can learn to hear silence in oral and written communications and inquire into its meanings; we can learn to hold silence as a means of resistance or as a way of communicating counter-majoritarian values; and we can teach with and about silence in order to introduce courtesies and modes of behavior that disrupt and subvert the dominant conventions."[15] Silence thus is made into a mode of resistance rather than a sign of complicity.

Collaborative learning is a core value in the critical classroom and beyond. The pedagogy of the traditional law school classroom reproduces "hierarchies of power and subordination" and "validates Euroheteropatriarchal perspectives."[16] To avoid that reproduction of hierarchy requires intentionality in teaching to minimize "privilege inside the classroom."[17] LatCrit scholars have illuminated how to create a classroom dynamic of collaborative learning:

> [C]ritical pedagogy ... intends to transform [traditional classroom] relationships of power by recognizing professors and students as co-creators of knowledge, unmasking the political and oppressive contents society imposes upon learners and teachers through hegemonic didactic practices, and formulating and incorporating more equitable methods of teaching in order to assist students and teachers to "develop consciousness of freedom, and connect knowledge to power." ...
>
> [T]he teachers' mission is not to deposit or pour knowledge into the brains of the learners, but to help uncover what they already know about the world. The ultimate goal is to uncover the *truth*.[18]

The LatCrit-infused classroom is thus "a democratic space that is emancipatory, creates conditions for learning, and fosters the critical exploration of society," with content taught "intentionally in a way that recognizes and minimizes privilege inside the classroom" and that "challenges the power differential between professors and students and fosters a horizontal teaching and learning community."[19]

LatCrit scholar Margaret Montoya, in particular, has emphasized the importance of community and connection in law school pedagogy, while maintaining "that voicing differences and helping students to understand their own role in racism and class domination is critical to making a pedagogy of community engagement meaningful."[20] LatCrit scholar Roberto Corrada adds that "an emancipatory pedagogy is one that is expansive, in the sense of including concern for students beyond the walls of a school or the boundaries of a school district, collaborative, in the sense of connecting to and working with people beyond our teaching peers or our faculty and whole, in the sense of engaging both mind and body—a traveling out to and communicating with people. A pedagogy of community engagement resonates with all of these ideas."[21]

Finally, as practiced within LatCrit, a critical pedagogy includes constant attention in the classroom to the knowledge of hidden histories that can supply a critical, contextual, multidimensional understanding of history and its legacy. Critical history illuminates how systemic injustice became legalized and remains entrenched. It often answers the "why" question for contemporary realities. Critical legal education is the tool students can use to pierce the veil of received knowledge and reclaim hidden truths as part of a social self-empowerment process.

Critical legal education provides a platform for unlearning and relearning systemic biases; once students educate themselves critically on the histories and legacies of "traditional" top-down identity politics in the United States, they can and do begin to discern the workings and patterns of systemic injustice. They then are better able to imagine themselves and act as antisubordination agents in law and society. The indispensable features of a critical legal education thus include (1) a consistent commitment to antisubordination knowledge and praxis (2) guided by contextualized understandings of hidden histories and (3) informed by critical and self-critical analysis of law and society.[22]

Two LatCrit community projects established during our first decade best exemplify in programmatic terms these shared and continuing ambitions. The first, the Cyber Classroom Project (CCP), supported by the University of Miami School of Law, was designed to help create, connect, and advance student reading groups based at various schools, especially those whose curricula were weak in critical theory offerings. Using a moderated listserv created for this purpose, the CCP allowed individuals and groups to set up discussion boards and engage each other across time and space for interschool exchanges. Periodically, or upon request, we provided suggested readings tailored to student interests. The second, the Critical Global Classroom, supported by the University of Baltimore School of Law, functioned as an accredited summer study-abroad program devoted to critical studies. This summer-long project offered students up to twelve academic credits for on-site studies in Chile, Argentina, and South Africa. Frequently, the International and Comparative Law Colloquium was embedded in the curriculum of the CGC, expanding student exposure to critical ideas and thinkers. Its largest enrollment reached eighty-plus students from law schools across the United States, as well as a handful from Global South schools. Moreover, this CGC group worked in tandem with the Cyber Classroom Project to nurture longer-term relationships and collaborations; after the summer ended, we invited and helped CGC students to remain in touch, and to meet new potential colleagues, via the CCP listserv. In different yet complementary ways, these two projects endeavored programmatically to transcend the physical, intellectual, and pedagogical boundaries of traditional legal education. From year to year, these projects and others helped bring students and teachers in personal touch with critical perspectives based on knowledge from the bottom of diverse social orders, especially those from the Global South.

In 2020, the devastation delivered by the COVID-19 pandemic reinvigorated, within both LatCrit and legal education more generally, attention to digital learning and technology. The challenge for LatCrit is to develop and offer curricula, likely based on the textbook discussed in the next section, that transcends the limits of the physical classroom and the faculty able and willing to teach an antisubordination-based curriculum while nonetheless building and maintaining community. In the same way that virtual technology offers the opportunity to develop conferences and discussions that transcend the material and temporal restrictions on travel by activist scholars, the challenge will be to establish and maintain the bond of connection and community that proximity has brought, whether in conferences or classrooms or the trenches of advocacy.

Targeting Systemic Injustice: The *Critical Justice* Textbook

> What does critical solidarity require now of us in terms of organizing and mobilizing? How do lawyers, organizers, academics, students, and allies move forward communally, centering systematic patterns of group injustice, preserving hard-fought gains from our ancestors, and forging ahead into a freer future? How can each of us best use our respective training and talents for this common struggle? What is the role of identity and education moving forward? What part will critical outsider jurisprudence and pedagogy have to play in formal and public education in the future? How do we make a difference now, and going forward, through personal and collective action?
>
> —Call for Papers, LatCrit XXI Biennial Conference

At the end of the LatCrit XV conference held in Denver during October 2010, West Publishing Company invited us, as a Board of Directors and community, to create a publication project that would include a textbook and accompanying online resources, including an online teaching wiki and guide. Unanimously, the board accepted the invitation and founded a project team to carry the work forward.[23] By 2011 the project team had begun meeting and LatCrit, as a tax-exempt nonprofit organization, had executed a contract with West ensuring that all royalties would go directly to the LatCrit community treasury. Over the years, this project became the *Critical Justice* textbook. In addition to creating an intellectual and pedagogical resource, we view this publication and teaching project as an opportunity to generate ongoing material resources for other community needs or goals.

In the ensuing decade, we managed to crystallize the textbook's[24] framing and main points as responses to critical, even existential, questions about law and justice (principally but not exclusively in the United States). The core queries and points include: How can contemporary advocates—lawyer or not—better use law to promote equal justice? How can contemporary advocates better apply the knowledge of lessons from history, experience, and theory regarding law and justice? In a world of *systemic* injustice, how do we make *systemic* progress? The answers to these core queries extend beyond law, but those answers cannot be pursued concretely without law.

In the early years, our work focused on coverage, concepts, content, and frameworks. Once we figured out the basic elements and highlights, the work turned more specifically to pedagogy, presentation, and syllabi. We struggled with different formats, sequences, and materials as we conducted workshops at schools, activist offices, and conferences to elicit feedback and improvements. Creating a textbook to fit a typical semester (in a U.S. law school or a university) while being thorough, organized, and user-friendly became the elusive goal, but it has been the focus of our efforts. Published in mid-2021 by West Academic Press, this ambitious project honors and builds on the histories and efforts that now enable this moment. As conceived and finalized, we hope this community-grounded and -cultivated textbook embodies LatCrit's values, functions, guideposts, postulates, and hallmarks regarding knowledge production and community-building.

While encompassing many sources, the general topics and framing of the textbook are reflected in its title: *Critical Justice: Systemic Advocacy in Law and Society.*[25] "Critical Justice," as the opening phrase, asserts the vision and object of the project: a condition of lived reality, both symbolically and materially, that ensures "equal justice for all" as measured from the "bottoms" of societal castes. The term also connotes the application of insights from the critical schools of legal knowledge, such as CRT and LatCrit, to interrogate the shortcomings of law and its complicity in persistent group inequalities. The term "Systemic" in the subtitle frames both the nature of persistent problems and of enduring solutions to them; it spells out the kind of *systemic* advocacy needed today. This kind of "Advocacy" invokes the imperative for lawyers and nonlawyers to act in concert and collaboration with organized groups, both within and more often beyond the courtroom. Finally, the subtitle's closing reference to "Law and Society" acknowledges that systemic injustice operates both internally and externally to law—that systemic injustice distorts law but injures society as well. To make and protect progress, systemic advocacy mixes community projects that build power to change the culture with legal projects that seek specific and enforced legal results through adjudication and/or policy-making.

The *Critical Justice* textbook is LatCrit's most significant contribution to critical knowledge and pedagogy in the classroom. As noted throughout this Primer, LatCrit through its SSP, FDW, and other programs has helped to expand the professoriate by mentoring student scholars and, once hired by the academy, by advancing and showcasing junior scholars. However, no LatCrit projects has addressed squarely the hypersubordination of law students through rising tuition/student debt and a shrinking job market—now, alongside the challenges beginning in 2020 of a pandemic economy. Neither could one organization alone tackle this juggernaut: the ideological training of law students to conform to elite power—coupled with the financial constraints of legal education, gatekeepers that include the bar exam, and the commodification of lawyers in the legal industry—all serve to handcuff change-minded law students to subservience and to service of elite interests. The *Critical Justice* textbook aims not only to highlight and unpack student debt as part of the legal industry but also to provide tools and techniques for organizing against the chains of student debt.

Although the *Critical Justice* textbook exposes and critiques the systemic constraints of traditional legal education and the legal industry, the challenge is to transform that education and industry to instead serve antisubordination aims and praxis. While neither LatCrit, nor anyone else, has succeeded in these goals, the challenge to legal education and the profession that the LatCrit community poses, as both insiders and outsiders, gives hope for transformation in the classroom and beyond. While an initial step, the teaching in law school classrooms, for academic credit, of a textbook that confronts the status quo of law as a system supporting inequality helps situate struggle squarely within the citadel. It aligns LatCrit goals with those of students committed to community goals of antisubordination praxis while they are trying to escape their own hypersubordination and handcuffs.

Given the textbook's contents and purposes, we hope that teachers interested in equal justice and an antisubordination future—whether in law or another context—will take a serious and lingering look at this substantial new resource. More than any other direct aim, this book strives to support social justice teachers in the classroom. And as noted above, adoption of the book can help support materially other community projects with similar aims. To help nudge this process institutionally, the LatCrit board has obligated itself to adopt this textbook and to help promote awareness of it:

> Oftentimes in LatCrit board or steering committee discussions, reminders are voiced that each board member owes a fiduciary duty to support the community/organization in every way feasible, whether monetarily, through devotion of time, through commitments and support from their home institutions, and through their creativity and skillsets. Although an organizational board member's duties of care and loyalty are sourced in law, for LatCrit they are more importantly sourced in ethics and responsibility. The latter sources reflect both the compelling global need for an antisubordination future, as well as the reality of how many board members benefitted individually, both the current and past boards, from their

engagement with LatCrit—professionally, personally, and otherwise, and in their teaching, their scholarship, and their praxis. . . .

. . . The LatCrit community, presumptively, should operate from the same baseline expectation that its community members are duty bound, as its board members are, to the fiscal, programmatic, creative, theoretical, coalitional, and mental health of the organization.[26]

These actions by the Board of Directors recognize that we, ourselves, constitute collectively our most important assets: our training, our skills, our energy, our criticality, our positions, and our privileges. These actions aim to become a starting point for supportive faculty across the academy and elsewhere to also adopt this textbook for an appropriate course as a matter of good pedagogy as well as a meaningful act of solidarity. Hopefully, over time, the initiative and example of LatCrit board members will motivate colleagues and other teachers to consider this innovative textbook for adoption in varied kinds of settings.[27]

The book itself aligns with the express centrality of justice in the mission statement and curriculum of most law schools and legal institutions. Equally important, adoption can (and should) align with the personal or professional goals of the teacher. To diversify its potential uses and benefits further, and thinking specifically of clinical or experiential education, the book emphasizes the practical *critical* skills necessary to using law for justice. To help systemic advocates get started, we show how to prepare applications for a variety of salaried postgraduate fellowships centered in social change lawyering. With the teacher's manual and online materials supporting those teaching the textbook, as well as syllabus development workshops planned for a variety of times and locations, new (or existing) courses using the book should be rewarding for all involved.

Unlike most every other textbook in the legal market, the three editors—two of whom are longtime board members of LatCrit—will receive no royalties; instead, all author revenues will be invested in the community treasury to support projects and diverse events. By adopting and teaching the textbook, each of us can help to make this critical community steadier and stronger. Moreover, by teaching these materials to students and future generations, each of us can contribute to the ranks of those able to challenge systemic injustice more effectively. Over the long haul, teaching or using these materials can help to empower tomorrow's critical pioneers.

7

Designing and Sustaining Self-Governance

Theory, Digital Presence, and Bricks and Mortar

Self-Governance for the Long Haul: Time, Change, and Progress

> The specific purposes of this corporation are to foster the development of Latina and Latino Critical Legal Theory [hereinafter referred to as "LatCrit" theory], to promote the dissemination of LatCrit scholarship, and to facilitate and enable the growth and further consolidation of the LatCrit [community] as a network of legal and interdisciplinary scholars, public interest lawyers and non-governmental organizations committed to the values of anti-subordination and inter-group and intra-group justice, both domestically and internationally.
>
> —LatCrit Articles of Incorporation, "Specific Purposes"

After the 1995 Puerto Rico colloquium on "Representing Latina/o Communities: Critical Race Theory and Practice," where LatCrit's naming took place, we focused our programmatic priorities on establishing an annual conference governed by the values, ethics, and principles we had come to share expressly.[1] The resulting LatCrit I conference began the practice of our shared, mutual commitments in collective and programmatic terms. At the end of that conference we had to decide how to proceed, if at all—questions decided the last morning, a Sunday, over a communal breakfast meeting open to all conference attendees. There we decided to organize a committee composed of organizers of the first conference, as well as new contributors, including some based at the site selected for the LatCrit II conference, San Antonio. Basically, we did the same for the following twenty-five years, trying always to balance veterans with newcomers in order to achieve collective memory and continuity as well as steady infusions of new energy, vision, and method. From these collaborative efforts to sustain the annual conference according to our common commitments, we branched out, attempting to do the same with the variety of projects we have initiated since 1995. Conference planning set the template for LatCrit self-governance as a community, producing a planning manual used flexibly for each conference since LatCrit V in Breckenridge, Colorado.[2]

From the outset, we also aimed to build a financial "nest egg" that each conference planning committee could pass on to help the following year's committee get a running start with hotel deposits and the like. This aim required our own bank account, which in turn required a formal name and structure. While working to sustain annual conferences through principled and accountable decisions, we realized the need for and benefits of nonprofit incorporation, a process that Elizabeth Iglesias shepherded.[3] This structure allowed us to manage finances autonomously and to coordinate the growing portfolio of projects in more synergistic ways, but it also required its own design, both formally and operationally.

Initially, our self-governance structure as a Florida nonprofit corporation included cochairs, project teams, and a Board of Directors. Essentially, every member of the board worked on at least one project, and the cochairs were supposed to help nurture the whole and plan for a longer-term future. Later, as described below, after a multiyear process of self-study and strategic planning, we overhauled our bylaws, in the process replacing the cochairs with the current self-governing framework: a Steering Committee with a restructured Board of Directors and project teams. The board meets in person twice annually—at the LatCrit or SALT alternating conferences and at the Annual Meeting of the American Association of Law Schools—and otherwise works year-round by phone, email, Zoom, and similar means. Project teams tend to do the same, or some variation, to complete their work. We have been struck time and again by how much progress we can make when meeting in person, so we value every LatCrit or similar program as a planning or governance opportunity.

As part of this diverse and fluid whole, the LatCrit approach to self-governance, like all our efforts, seeks to balance formality with critical rigor, all with an ethic of solidarity rooted in common commitments. Although we must comply of course with corporate formalities, we do so for the sake of helping to support bottom-up struggles for equal justice, both within the academy and beyond it. In this spirit, none of our LatCrit work is for pay; everyone volunteers what they want and can. Operationally, these institutional efforts necessarily grapple with the impediments of time, distance, resources, and other hurdles or limitations.

As explained in this Primer, our year-round events and virtual connections are intended to create a critical and inclusive zone of knowledge production and community-building, but they require much discussion and development—considerable time on the phone and computer. In addition to planning programs, conducting events, and nurturing publications, we began holding Board Planning Retreats and other kinds of similar gatherings to help chart and ground group directions; that is, to focus on self-governance. We held, for instance, Board-and-Friends Retreats every few years. Soon, these self-governance moments came to include the LatCrit Community Suite, which we host both at LatCrit events and other appropriate venues, including the AALS annual meeting. These suites allow conference-goers to congregate during the day and in the evening, informally as well as formally: every day the suite hosts small-scale meetings by LatCrit and friends, while in the evening the suite opens its doors to any conference participant, offering snacks and drinks to help everyone feel welcome and comfortable. During these times, participants meet new friends and reconnect with each other as they discuss program happenings, personal projects, and group plans, among other topics. Periodically, we hold a formal Community Forum in the suite to discuss creation of especially challenging or large projects, including the Junior Faculty Development Workshop, the Critical Global Classroom, the *Critical Justice* textbook, and the three-year self-study/strategic planning process concluded in 2010. The LatCrit Community Suite, as a recurrent project in itself, helps us to conduct current business while also generating and nourishing the relationships that sustain all other projects and the LatCrit enterprise as a cooperative whole. These suites are thick and active sites of community organization. They manifest, both informally and programmatically, how our projects help to enable the conditions for flexible, organized, and principled self-governance.

Exemplifying our self-governance practices, the Board of Directors in 2008 established a Task Force consisting of the most junior board members to study ourselves collectively and recommend changes (or not) relating to any aspect of the community. For three years, those Task Force members conducted surveys as well as interviews. They organized small-scale conversations embedded within the annual conference and other programs. It was a collective exercise in managing the passage of time, the complexity of change, and the need for progress. In the end, their work led to a revamping of LatCrit bylaws and the switch to a Steering Committee with a restructured Board and Project Teams.[4] It also set the stage for a proactive process for a generational transition in LatCrit self-governance that was complete by 2018.

LatCrit, as an entity, adopted the corporate form with the critical consciousness that corporate actors generally pursue interests at odds with equal justice, but also that these actors enjoy benefits under law vital even to organizations seeking transformative change and implementing antisubordination values. In the case of LatCrit, the primary benefit to nonprofit status was access to the privileged federal tax designation as a 501(c)(3) nonprofit corporation, with tax deductibility to its donors.[5] This designation enables LatCrit to compete with traditional nonprofits for donor money, with the fundamental difference that in contrast to most nonprofits whose day-to-day governance and decision-making are conducted through sometimes highly paid administrators, as explained above, LatCrit's governing bodies are not compensated by the organization, which enables donations to inure fully to the benefit of community projects. Indeed, many of those LatCrit volunteers additionally have contributed significant financial resources toward the organization from their own funds. We encourage readers and community members to take account of this difference in their own ongoing donation decisions and actions.[6] As a whole, the continuing history of designing and administering LatCrit, Inc., as an active and ethical (volunteer) entity amounts to a community effort to walk the talk—in and out of the classroom.

Digital Presence: Technology as Resource and Challenge

Increasingly, the power to communicate is determined by access to, control of, or authority over the means of communication. Indeed, the "means of communication" have become as central to the structure of power/lessness in our postmodern, hyperlinked, globalized, mass media society as the "means of production" were central to the class struggles of modernizing industrialism.
—Elizabeth Iglesias[7]

LatCrit efforts to create online resources commenced in the early years and have continued since then. Our first website was hosted at the University of Florida College of Law and administered by Pedro Malavet. Its creation coincided with our early annual conferences to allow us to provide the program schedule to all interested persons. The plan for the website was to make registration for LatCrit conferences easier for everyone, as well as to begin an archive of LatCrit programs and publications. Eventually it would become a tool of knowledge and organizing.

Within a couple of years, the website migrated to the University of Miami School of Law and then the University of Denver Sturm College of Law, where we expanded the contents and upgraded the software. Eventually, the website migrated to the University of Connecticut, where Charles Venator-Santiago and others undertook a multiyear effort to update the contents and software again. This collective process presented many opportunities to expand our work, but also many challenges. As academics, few of us have sufficient technical knowledge to make the most of online resources. And our funding is limited. Nonetheless, we have done our collective best over the years. Today, our community website at www.latcrit.org is administered independently and directly by the LatCrit Board and Steering Committee, with technical assistance from supportive vendors and a reliance on community funds for its continual renewal and upgrading—with the latest such renewal and reconception taking place throughout 2020. Among other modernizations and enhancements, this major upgrade infused the website with a variety of photos from past events, going beyond the sampling provided in this Primer and in living color.

Substantively, the website is organized to serve informational as well as archival purposes. At any given moment, the website offers current information about upcoming or planned events and programs, such as the biennial LatCrit Conference, the annual Faculty Development Workshop, the Student Scholar Program, the South-North Exchange, and other projects described in this Primer. But the website also provides access to previous events and programs, as well as to past publications. To make access as easy as possible for users anywhere in the world, the website either provides links to the contents of previous LatCrit symposia or provides the full articles directly on our site. Similarly, the website provides current as well as historical information, including images, about our various projects, including some projects not discussed elsewhere in this Primer.

For example, the Oral Histories Project is a series of recorded video interviews conducted during the LatCrit XII annual conference in

Miami Beach designed to provide a snapshot of that moment in our collective history from the perspective of varied participants. Similarly, the Syllabi Bank Project is a collection of syllabi used by teachers around the country for various courses so that new (and all) teachers can compare approaches, readings, and highlights to improve the quality of education generally. We invite readers to visit the LatCrit website periodically for both historical and current information about these and other community initiatives.

A particularly significant part of the website is the Scholarship Research Toolkit described below. This toolkit provides an index to all LatCrit symposia organized by themes and keywords. We update this toolkit periodically, most recently in early 2021, to include the latest publications.

Building on this website, in recent years a Facebook presence and Twitter account were established and maintained by Saru Matambanadzo and others, which we invite all community members to use. These represent our first efforts to take advantage of social media as a tool of critical knowledge and antisubordination solidarity, while mindful it is being used at the same time as a tool to perpetuate existing inequities. As with the website itself, we do the best we can with social media—given our resources, challenges, and constraints. As with the LatCrit experiment as a whole, these efforts remain perpetually under construction; we invite all interested persons to join us in any way they can to improve the odds for equal justice.

[N]ew modern modes of scholarly and collegial interaction should be explored as platforms to supplant or enhance elements of the traditional LatCrit conference template. For example, how can synchronous and asynchronous interactive online video bring together LatCrit community members for scholarly and other professional exchanges and collaborations in-between in-person gatherings? How could a LatCrit You Tube channel ("LatCritTV," say) help us? What about social media? Could a

#LatCrit hashtag and an invigorated Facebook account organizing all of our members, as two modest examples, facilitate more communication and interaction while raising LatCrit's visibility online?

—Anthony E. Varona[8]

One of the challenges and shortcomings of LatCrit's presence online and through social media is the delivery thus far of most content in the English language. Many LatCrit community members are native fluent in Spanish, and some of the activists in the Americas with whom we interact speak Indigenous languages. Most conference presentations, programs, website materials, and social media content have been delivered in English. Among other reasons, English, even if the second (or even third) language of many of our community members, is nonetheless the most widely understood common language within the community. But we do our best. For example, a few of our symposia publications include Spanish-language texts,[9] and the CLAVE journal discussed in chapter 4, published jointly with the UIAPR, is written almost exclusively in Spanish. In many oral LatCrit conference presentations, participants either self-translate or language-switch between English and Spanish for a cultural concoction that brings *realidad* and *corazón* to the conference environment. Almost from the start, we have used translation technology to supply SNX participants with radio-frequency earbuds to listen to a simultaneous translation from Spanish to English or vice versa; the most recent 2018 South-North Exchange in Antigua, Guatemala, used community-purchased equipment available for future events.

Our experience with the intersection of language, culture, and technology suggests we can do better. Better to confront and disrupt traditional language norms within the academy. Better to translate the content of our online website and social media presence into language(s) other than English.[10] Better to acknowledge that some in our community may be hearing-challenged at our oral conferences and vision-challenged in accessing the written content of our knowledge production. We can rely, in part, on technology to bridge these gaps while ever mindful and alert that technology exists not to build the solidarity we seek but to make profit; therefore, our community interests and those of technology may converge, but that alliance is contested and, like the LatCrit experiment, remains under construction.

Most recently, the widespread conversion to online legal education due to COVID-19 allows us to imagine and assemble a critical curriculum in our community website that makes critical knowledge more accessible to more people. This curriculum could be fashioned from the courses already being modified for online education. It can include mini-courses based on the *Critical Justice* textbook outlined in chapter 6. It can help students, faculty, activists, organizers, and others to supplement their own work and knowledge. As with all online education, we can combine synchronous, asynchronous, and hybrid courses to suit topics and circumstances. Over this third decade, LatCrit can help to create a resource and repository of critical actionable knowledge that few others are able, or interested, to do. The existing Research Toolkit, discussed next and already built into the community website, provides a starting point.

[T]he first LatCrit meeting, which took place in conjunction with the Hispanic National Bar Association's Annual Meeting, was held in Puerto Rico—the island paradise where I was raised in an extended, loving family. In order to attend the gathering and hear our presentations, Mami y papi flew down from Miami. . . . When it was time for me to speak I, imperceptibly to all but myself, traveled a million worlds in a matter of moments. Because mi familia was there, I was forced deliberately, consciously, premeditatedly to choose a language for my presentation. . . . So there I was . . . speaking at a Hispanic Bar meeting to a room full of Latina and Latino law professors, having had mi familia travel to see me talk about Latinas and Latinos and our communities, unable to use my mother tongue—the language with which they raised me, one that they will understand—for to do so would have resulted in the exclusion of many of my colleagues.

—Berta E. Hernández-Truyol[11]

Scholarship Research Toolkit: Accessing and Using Knowledge

Recommendation 14: Revise all publication submission guidelines to require greater engagement with LatCrit scholarship.

—LatCrit Board of Directors Self-Study[12]

Early in LatCrit's history as a scholarly movement, LatCrit scholars recognized the importance of engaging and building on the existing body of OutCrit and LatCrit discourses.[13] LatCrit scholars collectively acknowledged this imperative by compiling a Primer of foundational LatCrit scholarship in uncut, full-length form, distributed annually to conference participants, initially in hardcopy, then on disk, and eventually through the LatCrit website. Our expectation was that conference participants in their various roles as speakers, writers, and discussants, particularly those from other disciplines, would better engage with the conference themes when familiar with our history and scholarly publications.

As the LatCrit body of published symposia grew through the years, however, the limits of the unedited, unabridged Primer model became evident. Capturing the burgeoning body of LatCrit work, and introducing scholars both new and old to LatCrit's "cohesive yet sprawling enterprise," now required more user-friendly and targeted tools. Responding to these needs, the LatCrit community developed and made available on its website in 2010 a vital innovation toward the production of OutCrit scholarship.

That resource—the LatCrit Scholarship Research Toolkit—consists of two different indices, one thematic and the other based on keywords and terms. Both are online as part of the LatCrit website and are designed to be distinct though complementary. The Thematic Index focuses on more than two dozen substantive themes (collected in appendix G of this book) of published LatCrit scholarship derived from the nearly fifty symposia that LatCrit scholars have produced and published since 1995. In effect, the Thematic Index tracks the efforts of LatCrit theorists to explore and elucidate these general categories of inquiry across a number of years, with each essay or article published in a LatCrit symposium assigned to and arranged by one or more of these themes.

In addition, the LatCrit Keyword Index organizes the articles from LatCrit symposia by specific keywords designed to provide easy entry points for research of this considerable literature. In addition to many other terms or concepts, these keywords include starting points based on geography, critical schools and frameworks of thought, and identities organized by various categories. Not surprisingly, many of the keywords overlap with the terms comprising the themes of the Thematic Index, but the Keyword Index also provides an extended list of more precise categories that thoroughly map the symposium pieces.

Building on the resources available through www.latcrit.org, the Research Toolkit offers the LatCrit community the opportunity to search, discover, and create a window to the past and present of Lat-Crit scholarship uniquely tailored to their specific needs and interests. Both indices aim to help researchers, but each takes a slightly different approach, hoping to help diverse researchers expedite their work. The generality of the Thematic Index lends itself, for example, to comparative and interdisciplinary work and allows broader comparison of existing scholarship, while the Keyword Index ensures any LatCrit scholar can track or access the specific concepts or issues taken on by LatCrit theorists. The main difference between the two is the level of generality—the themes listed are more generalized than the fairly specific keywords. As a general rule, pieces earmarked simultaneously in similar ways by both indices indicate that the researcher or reader definitely should engage those pieces when traversing a similar scholarly path. At all times, researchers and readers should mix and match elements of each index to suit their purposes and provide the surest scope of results.

As much as possible, both the Thematic Index and the Keyword Index are designed to be user-friendly. In addition to searching by theme and/ or keyword, users can search the literature by date of publication and by author name. Thus, every researcher or reader can easily customize their uses of this database for maximum efficiency and benefit.

The community's hope and expectation for all readers and researchers interested in LatCrit knowledge production is that they will engage the rich and deep body of published LatCrit works with the aid of this toolkit, rather than reading or writing on a clean canvas divorced from this communal body of work. Indeed, this scholarly hope and expectation is embedded in the fifth LatCrit guidepost, which calls for appreciating, incorporating, and applying the jurisprudential past to everything we undertake. If you have a computer or device at hand, take a moment to peruse and familiarize yourself with this accessible resource—and then be prepared to use it to streamline and enhance your own critical research, reading, and writing in the future.

Theory, Bricks, and Mortar: Campo Sano and Living Justice

Having an independent physical base has become critical as universities and law schools increasingly are even less equipped to focus on legal problems of the poor and the "outsiders" of society due to increasing budgetary, bureaucratic and political constraints. After sixteen years of laying the groundwork for this bricks-and-mortar move, [LatCrit's] "Living Justice Institute" located in the middle of [Florida] will enable LatCrits to take their teaching, learning and writing projects on behalf of the underprivileged to the next level of sustainability and effectiveness.

—LatCrit website[14]

In 2011, after the three-year self-study and strategic planning process described above,[15] the LatCrit Board approved the acquisition of a ten-acre parcel (named by the community as Campo Sano, meaning "wellness camp," with the full name of Campo Sano—The LatCrit Community Campus) to create a permanent community center and campus for LatCrit scholars and affiliated networks. Campo Sano is located in DeLeon Springs in central Florida. The principal structure is a 3,000-square-foot artist's retreat with spaces for formal and informal small-scale events. Three years later, in 2014, the LatCrit community established the Living Justice Institute (LJI) at Campo Sano as a democratic base and diverse hub; a safe and supportive haven for multiply-diverse groups and persons, working collaboratively and ethically toward a postsubordination future, on multiple levels of human endeavor. We structured this new institute as an academic organization to spearhead innovation, as well as continuity, in the perpetual advancement of the core social and educational purposes, principles, and practices developed by LatCrit and other OutCrit scholars since the 1990s. By design, the LJI at Campo Sano is grounded in critical theory, coalitional community, and antisubordination praxis.

In addition to the continual advancement of LatCrit's basic societal goals and knowledge-production activities, we dedicated the LJI at Campo Sano to the nourishment of human and environmental dignity, well-being, society, and harmony in every respect: mind, body, spirit, and soul. The creation of the LJI at Campo Sano situates critical antisubordination networks within and beyond the U.S. legal academy to work and live justice in holistic, integrated, and multigenerational ways. Ideally, Campo Sano increasingly will provide a safe, peaceful setting for the cultivation of critical communities and coalitions based on shared social justice commitments. Through the work of the LJI and affiliated persons or partners, Campo Sano offers a self-sustaining and self-directed sanctuary to incubate decolonizing knowledge and consciousness, foster egalitarian human society, and engender activist academic democracy for generations to come.

During the first several years of this physical, intellectual, and spiritual project, we emphasized the creation of common areas and the construction of a new structure for our activities. We also began a community-wide series of conversations to help prioritize the directions we should take with this new, unique resource. We have conducted this wide-ranging multilogue programmatically in plenary settings like the LatCrit conferences and other programs, but also informally in numerous smaller gatherings. Currently, the planning envisions our next steps in development of the grounds and facilities, as well as an increasingly active schedule of diverse small-scale events consistent with the LJI Mission Statement (excerpted in appendix H), including events conducted by local groups as may be best for them. Constrained by time and other resources (both material and human), this community discussion continues. Even so, varied groups and individuals have begun to hold programs, meetings, retreats, and workshops there, including the LatCrit board.

These programs and workshops took root in the biennial conference gatherings. For example, in October 2017, during the biennial LatCrit conference in Orlando, a large number of conference attendees visited Campo Sano and exchanged views about potential uses of this Community Campus. One result of this visit was a firm plan for a recurring writing workshop honoring and deploying the methods of LatCrit "pioneer" Margaret Montoya to help incubate a new generation of knowledge production. In May 2018, LatCrit, in partnership with the LJI, held the first annual Margaret Montoya Writing Workshop at Campo Sano. The following year, 2019, we did the same and, with the exception of the 2020 pandemic summer, plan to continue this relatively new project in the coming years.

This project's main objective is to foster and support junior critical scholars and teachers in cultivating together the kind of intellectually imaginative scholarship that Professor Montoya and other LatCrit veterans contributed to the academy. A small, intensive event, this annual writing workshop includes between ten and twenty scholars at various

FIGURE 7.1. Margaret Montoya Writing Workshop, May 2018, Campo Sano

FIGURE 7.2. LatCrit Board and Friends Retreat, October 2017, Campo Sano

stages of their careers, with junior faculty, fellows, and students especially encouraged to participate as a source of professional development and scholarly support. Through this mentoring, the workshop adds a new venue for our pipelining and community-building efforts across generations of scholars and scholarship.

Additionally, the broad LatCrit community has started taking initiatives to use our Community Campus. For example, in February 2020, some attendees of the Montoya writing workshops organized a Writing & Solidarity Retreat at Campo Sano attended by emerging critical scholars from across Florida. And the board, or some of the project teams, also have met there. But, on the whole, Campo Sano remains underused; one of our current aims is to change that fact. For now, with and through activities like these, LatCrit and related networks of scholars, activists, educators, and change-agents rededicate the bricks, mortar, and spirit of LJI at Campo Sano to producing a better, more equal world for all.

How the still unfolding repercussions of the COVID-19 pandemic will affect these (or other) plans remains in question at the time of publication, although like many other organizations LatCrit has continued to hold planned events or meetings online using platforms like Zoom. One initial response, of course, has been to refocus attention and resources on upgrading our community website and online capabilities, building on efforts like those described above in this chapter. Although most everything remains unclear in this first year of the pandemic, one key point is already clear for LatCrit: we must figure out how to create synergies between bricks and mortar and online capacity. While gathering in person face-to-face remains our ideal, we have to innovate ways that maximize Campo Sano's uses while also building our online resources and events. In this (post-)COVID era, the connection between the material and the virtual has to be reviewed and revamped, and bridged proactively and synergistically, for the longer run.

8

Looking Ahead

Staying Nimble Yet Grounded

Generations and Transitions: Using Continuity to Build Progress

Conceived in 1995, LatCrit has reached well-established maturity—a well-rooted, well-bred adulthood. Yet LatCrit remains young, and precocious, and even adolescent, in the best sense of that word. Its view of itself and of the world is still evolving, and fresh.

—Anthony E. Varona

LatCrit's system of rotating centers, shifting bottoms, and streams of programming depends on a collective yet individual commitment to continuity and progression. Because rotation in part means that each event in a stream builds on those of the prior one(s), LatCrit programs and projects place a premium on repeat attendance and participation in its events. To engineer the continual advancement of this discourse, knowledge, and community, rotation calls for a personal and annual re/commitment to the LatCrit enterprise among an ever fluid yet identifiable and self-selected group of scholars. But no one can be everywhere all the time. The forms of commitment and participation among the many individuals in the LatCrit community vary over time, of course. Generally, however, this commitment to participation encompasses not only attendance and presentations but also planning and administrative work. The goal is to ensure a critical mass of continuity in attendance, participation, and planning—and then to balance these levels of continuity and consolidation with innovation, expansion, and inclusion.

This complex balancing of continuity and development must antici-
pate and accommodate the varying levels of knowledge and experience
that individual scholars bring with them to LatCrit events: inevitably, different individuals bring with them not only varied backgrounds but also
varied levels of exposure to, or involvement in, critical or outsider jurisprudence. This accommodation contains both substantive and structural
components: it is reflected in LatCrit programs, which seek to blend the
familiar with the novel and to represent both newcomers and veterans.
Difficult though it is, the perpetual task of the group is to create an environment where all present can participate and contribute, a task that necessarily becomes increasingly challenging with the group's expansion.[1]

Only time—and effort—will determine how far LatCrit's capacity
for academic activism will (or won't) reach. The ultimate challenge, of
course, is to persist for as long as the material conditions of subordination also persist. For the moment, it seems to be working because
enough OutCrit scholars deem it worthwhile. The immediate and
ongoing challenge, as always, is to locate, excavate, and rotate sites of
theoretical contestation and political action to keep the LatCrit antisubordination project continuously on balance and on the move.

To help ensure this ongoing evolution, the LatCrit board and community proactively invite newer ranks of faculty to participate in programs
and project teams with a view toward taking charge of them. As the
three-year self-study and strategic planning process helped to demonstrate, these collective long-term efforts aim to support continuity *and*
progression beyond any person or cohort. These community efforts
specifically helped in recent years to support a generational transition
in LatCrit governance structures that balances experience with fresh-
ness. As a result, by 2018 LatCrit governance of itself and its projects was
in the hands of a new and diverse generation.[2] This kind of forward-
looking transition, we hope, will be repeated time again in the coming
years (and perhaps decades).

To help ensure it, we must personally and programmatically support
critical knowledge production throughout all stages of a career—from

student to novice teacher to scarred veteran. This support includes helping students to minimize debt and its disabling effects, as well as helping all faculty to evolve as activist teachers and scholars through different career stages. We must help to create opportunities for knowledge and advancement without indenturing the next generation even before they graduate; and we must also create more opportunities for elders and veterans to share their experiences—our histories—so that every generation can better understand, defend, and build on past gains. In today's socially distanced context, designing and offering online courses and events, like those described above in chapter 7, is one doable, significant contribution that this community can tackle. By summer 2020, LatCrit programming had shifted, at least temporarily, to a fully online format, with FDW sessions (including one on job callbacks in a COVID-19 world) and monthly substantive, praxis-oriented panels and discussions taking place over Zoom. That discussion series—titled "LatCrit Fridays: A Virtual Symposium Series: Policing, Pandemics, Praxis & Power"— addressed subjects in fall 2020 ranging from identity-laden abuses in policing and pandemic health consequences to the 2020 election and praxis interventions going forward.

LatCrit's new *Critical Justice* textbook, described in chapter 6, looks to upcoming generations of activist students and lawyers to defend and expand past breakthroughs. As detailed in chapter 5, for LatCrit community members much of that praxis has been focused on interjecting bottom-up perspectives everywhere we could. Within the U.S. legal academy, we built a "home" that structurally fits within the system but that intellectually and operationally upends it. It remains a still-fragile and evolving experiment. Although we have not transformed academia, we have demonstrated an alternative that, in the present, ameliorates the dangers of the academy and elsewhere. As the *Critical Justice* text elaborates, even short-term ameliorative measures, which consume so much time and energy in the moment, can point toward a postsubordination future; amelioration can be designed for transformation when connected to community projects that build the capacity for collective actions in the long term. LatCrit, as a fluid yet cohesive community, is committed to this end in all it undertakes.

In brief, the challenge for present and future generations is to be nimble yet to stay grounded. Nimbleness alone can be purposeless and lead to drift. Grounding in values and principles alone can become formulaic and can lead to rigidity. We need both, in flexibly balanced combinations, to make a difference that matters and endures in the volatile relationship of law to justice. Awareness of circumstance, context, and change requires us to be nimble—to be always ready to adapt, innovate, and improve. At the same time, principle and accountability require us to remain grounded in the express commitments we have made to ourselves and to each other. Nimbleness and grounding thus require self-criticality—an open-minded willingness to assess honestly, openly, and rigorously, and to change accordingly, our own work. They entail moments of uncertainty, even disagreement and conflict, which ideally become opportunities to correct errors, transcend self-limitations, and reduce shortcomings. Nimbleness and grounding, together, help us to act for the long haul in critically ethical ways that advance the integrity and relevance of our work.

To be both nimble and grounded requires us to know our own histories and trajectories, including our gains, limits, and losses, so that we may better understand how we got here and where we stand going forward. This balancing requires us to understand the current moment in historical and systemic terms so that we may better envision and enact a more free and equal future. This perspective and knowledge help us to figure out what *we* should do next, given all that came before. Progress requires us to know and to act collaboratively based on experience *and* on vision, across multiple vectors of difference, to advance the shared objective of equal justice for all. And the new, morphing challenges posed by the COVID-19 pandemic put an extra premium on these longstanding basics.

LatCrit's focus is Latino/a, but its embrace is universal. . . . As an academic identity and a scholarly brand, LatCrit is a powerhouse. But it, like so many other children of the 1990s—does not readily conform to

LOOKING AHEAD | 111

the last century's labels. It is a theoretical movement, an organization, an association of scholars, that valorizes purpose and connection, utility and impact. LatCrit did not fit nor even break the mold of the academic movements that preceded it. Molds restrict, and confine the future to the vision and margins of the past. LatCrit by contrast, always has been beyond molds and, instead, has fixed its focus on the future, and what can be envisioned, and manifested, through critical legal theory combined with focused collective action. LatCrit has shape-shifted through the decades to respond to the practical needs of its members and the academy.
—Anthony E. Varona[3]

The relatively young LatCrit record (as compared to the centuries-long arc of ongoing subordinations) thus posits collective, programmatic action as indispensable both to knowledge production and to social struggle and has proceeded from this premise to construct the conditions that would enable it in the varied jurisprudential, institutional, geographic, and social settings that we inhabit. Recognizing the challenges to ethical praxis and academic democracy encountered by our jurisprudential ancestors and precursors, LatCrit has minted concepts and developed tools to align individual commitments and collective undertakings in substantively principled and accountable terms. Whether or not these unfolding efforts toward the shared ultimate goal of a postsubordination social order will endure remains to be seen. In the meantime, this fragile experiment, movement, and community known as "LatCrit" continues its self-organizing, activist march through this third decade; despite limitations, mistakes, and shortcomings, we still march on.[4]

Substantive Agendas: Critical Approaches to Hemispheric Justice Studies[5]

[LatCrit] transnational events and publications are likewise designed to produce the same goals as the conferences

and symposia—knowledge and community, and community solidarity through shared knowledge—but specifically and squarely in hemispheric and global framings. These border-crossing efforts, which are designed to convene outside the U.S. in diverse locations, ideally help, over time, to create multilateral pipelines for increasingly globalized participation in our conferences and entire Portfolio of Projects and an increasingly globalized community of academic activists who are ready, willing, and able to act in principled solidarity toward a post-subordination society in varied locations and settings.
—Sarudzayi M. Matambanadzo, Francisco Valdes & Sheila Velez[6]

Given the shared, though varied, histories of conquest and colonization across the hemisphere, and their attendant ideologies, our programmatic efforts to date necessarily have included critical examinations of patriarchy, Eurocentrism, white supremacy, and homophobia as interconnected social ills that systematically deform the lives of many citizens across many neo/colonial societies, regions, and eras. Thus, much like critical outsider jurisprudence focused mostly in/on the United States, LatCrit's approaches to hemispheric justice studies must interrogate and challenge systemic injustice in its local as well as its global expressions. In this way—and perhaps only through these ways—can critical networks of activist antisubordination scholars help to produce the knowledge necessary to sustain social action to dismantle transnationally the centuries-old edifice of identity castes. Shared critical knowledge, as we have discussed above, can foster coalitional antisubordination solidarity across multiple kinds of difference or borders.

Undertaking a sustained, collective, programmatic development of critical approaches to hemispheric justice studies provides a substantive, focused, and expansive agenda for coming generations of LatCrit and OutCrit scholars. Activating critical South-North networks to pursue this cross-bordered, long-term agenda is the next and pressing step in the development of an outsider counter-tradition to academic imperialism in and through hemispheric justice studies. As imagined here, and as reflected in the themes, programs, and publications of the SNX, ICC, and similar LatCrit projects since the mid-1990s, hemispheric justice studies would encompass at least five overlapping lines of critical inquiry and socio-legal action:

- The first line inquiry and action is to establish constitutional governance at all levels of organized society based on inclusive, participatory democracy accountable and responsive to the general public interest.
- Next, and related, is the securing and self-determination of Native, Indian, and First Nation societies and the reparation of stolen lands and resources to them.
- Third is the enforcement of economic justice, both in "domestic" and international relations, to ensure the dignity, well-being, and basic livability of all humans across socioeconomic strata.
- The fourth set of concerns involves the efficacious protection of human rights, ranging from the political to the social, cultural, and collective, regardless of class, race, sex, sexual orientation, gender identity, religion, culture, citizenship, or other kinds of human identities.
- Finally, the substantive agenda of critical approaches to hemispheric justice studies would encompass respect for the planet as a common human resource that no individual, group, or corporation has the right to exploit at will and would strive to control private profiteering at public expense.

Of course, these five points of substantive engagement reflect the baseline political economies that sustain the institutions and structures of hemispheric injustice. It thus bears emphasis that these five sets of antisubordination concerns present a long-term substantive agenda for hemispheric justice studies and related actions or reforms. After all, the present-day architecture of Euroheteropatriarchy took a half-millennium to emplace across the hemisphere (and throughout many other parts of the globe); reversing and dismantling the neocolonial status quo necessarily is a multigenerational project. At this (and every) stage, *our* task is to build on the record established thus far to the best of our individual and collective capacities and to pay forward the gains of the past.

El Espíritu de Resistencia

SUMI CHO AND ANGELA P. HARRIS

We are delighted and honored by the opportunity to reflect on LatCrit's past, present, and future in this afterword. Like Margaret Montoya's foreword to this Primer, our story begins in the present, with the stunning cascade of public debates and confrontations organized and held, in part, by the coalition called the Movement for Black Lives (M4BL): the worldwide street protests, the public confrontations and conversations within venerable arts, entertainment, and media organizations, the toppling of statues, and the explosions of Black joy.

In the "Who We Are" section of its website, M4BL describes itself in language that resonates with many of the principles and commitments that have been outlined in this book:

- We are Abolitionist:
  - We believe that prisons, police and all other institutions that inflict violence on Black people must be abolished and replaced by institutions that value and affirm the flourishing of Black lives.
  - We believe in centering the experiences and leadership of the most marginalized Black people, including but not limited to those who are trans and queer, women and femmes, currently and formerly incarcerated, immigrants, disabled, working class, and poor.

- We believe in transformation and a radical realignment of power:
  The current systems we live inside of need to be radically
  transformed, which includes a realignment of global power. We
  are creating a proactive, movement-based vision instead of a
  reactionary one.
- We build kinship with one another:
  - We draw from political lessons, grow in our leadership, and expanding
    our base to build a stronger movement.
- We are anti-capitalist:
  - We believe and understand that Black people will never achieve libera-
    tion under the current global racialized capitalist system.[1]

Like M4BL, LatCrit has promoted a critical, transformative antiracist vision and sought to build a movement of fellow travelers "for
the long haul." Take, for example, LatCrit's ideological approach to
knowledge building. As LatCrit's logo—the "upside down" globe—
indicates, as an organization it has been dedicated to destabilizing the
conventional international margins/periphery divide. For decades,
as Francisco Valdes and Steven Bender document here, LatCrit has
embraced community-building based on solidarity and has treated
heterogeneity within its ranks as a strength: looking always to center those excluded or on the margins and linking subjects inhabiting
social categories of exclusion or outsiderness based on commonality
of shared structures of subordination as well as shared solidarities of
resistance.

Yet, we see LatCrit not simply as spiritual fellow travelers with the
Movement for Black Lives. Unlike M4BL, LatCrit—an organization
composed mostly of tenure-track law professors—was founded and operates within a bastion of the U.S. professional-managerial class: academia. In this afterword, we examine how the contradictions inherent
to this political-economic location have shaped LatCrit's past successes
and create challenges to its future.

LatCrit's Beginnings

LatCrit emerged at an expansive moment in the academy. State support for public universities was still robust, and tuition at private institutions was rising in tandem with the liberal availability of student loans. Law schools were doing a brisk business, and on many campuses they provided revenue streams that subsidized administration and less lucrative departments and programs. Law schools in the 1990s had also begun to embrace the symbolic politics of "diversity."[2]

With respect to diversity hiring, law schools had a lot of catching up to do. In the late 1980s, the top fifteen law schools (according to the maligned yet slavishly followed *US News and World Report* rankings[3]) had only token representation of people of color and few to no Latinx faculty.[4] To illustrate how commonplace the utter absence or paucity of faculty of color was at U.S. law schools nationwide, consider that, in 1986–1987, more than half of law schools surveyed—75 out of 144, or 52 percent—had *either zero or only one racial minority* among their faculty, defined as "black, Hispanic and others, such as Asians and Native Americans."[5] Although racial integration of student bodies had begun in public K–12 schools in the 1950s, and spread to higher education by the late 1960s and 1970s, the pressure to racially diversify did not begin to affect law school faculties until the late 1980s and 1990s.[6] Faculty of color hired before 1990 (with the exception of the HBCUs and universities in Puerto Rico) were therefore racial unicorns, working in isolation and with little support[7] and often hired only after a predecessor faculty member of color in the department had retired or died.

Thanks in part to continued student and faculty advocacy, law schools in the late 1980s began to be prodded away from the unicorn model of hiring and promotion. Progress moved in fits and starts: too many law schools simply transitioned to what could be called a "Noah's Ark" model, in which one male and one female of a given racial minority group was the goal and effective ceiling. Part of the challenge of diversification during these desegregation years was redefining what it meant to be "qualified." For example, although Feminist Legal Theory and Critical Race Theory—along with other intellectual "law-and" movements such as "law and society" and "law and humanities"—had expanded the definition of legal scholarship beyond narrowly doctrinal work (an expansion welcomed by many a student law review editor), advocates for minority hiring still had to do battle with and around the conventional qualifications without which nonwhite candidates always appeared "risky": a U.S. Supreme Court or appellate court clerkship, law review editorship, membership in the Order of the Coif. Advocates for minority hires, and the new hires themselves, had to assuage their white colleagues' anxiety that any move toward "diversity" automatically threatened "excellence" as defined by the narrow, traditional standards under which the old guard had been hired and promoted.

Nonetheless, in the 1990s the academic tenure track was, overall, smoother and wider than it had ever been. If law school professorships did not pay as well as jobs at large law firms, they nonetheless offered autonomy, prestige, flexibility of working conditions, job satisfaction, job security, and ample salaries compared to the incomes of the average American. Indeed, thanks to the market-based "opportunity cost" argument, law professors made substantially more than their peers in other academic departments. Once you got hired (and managed the perilous transition to tenure), life as a law professor was pretty good.

LatCrit, therefore, emerged with a fundamental contradiction: pursuing a radical project as members of an extremely privileged elite. It's perhaps not surprising that, over time, LatCrit's more radical ambitions toward transformative change were sanded down, and its greatest success appears to have been as a professional organization seeking greater inclusion—a decidedly liberal, not radical, accomplishment. Yet, these are the challenges that confront many organizations engaging in collective struggle: How to institutionalize radical ambitions to ensure continuity? How to develop future leaders while avoiding "founders' disease"?

How to foster inclusiveness and low barriers to entry while discouraging rampant opportunism or substantive drift from first principles?

Consider LatCrit's successes in the last twenty-five years. First, Lat-Crit, working alongside other professional organizations, helped change the demographics of law school faculties, demanding and getting far more diversification than what would have otherwise occurred. LatCrit developed pipeline programs—the Student Scholar Program and the Faculty Development Workshop—to prepare candidates for the academic job market. Indeed, through its Student Scholar Program, LatCrit opened its doors (literally) to students, welcoming them to attend and even present at its annual/biennial conferences. LatCrit also participated in political movements to change the conditions of possibility for hiring faculty from groups, backgrounds, and perspectives unlike those populating overwhelmingly homogenous law faculties that were de rigueur through at least the 1980s. Mindful of the problem of hiring, tenuring, and promotion, LatCrit also developed an extensive advocacy network of support, calling as needed upon informal "stewards" at nearly every ABA-accredited law school.

Second, in addition to increasing the physical presence of underrepresented faculty, LatCrit helped bring about a turn in the definition of acceptable scholarship. As eminent critical race scholars had done before them, LatCrit scholars expanded the acceptable topics, approaches, and methods for legal scholarship, paving the way for new entrants to further redefine their fields. Substantive areas of particular concern to Latinx populations—such as globalization, immigration, settler colonialism, neocolonialism, and language rights—percolated and "found voice" at LatCrit conferences. Works-in-progress sessions built into Lat-Crit conferences provided substantive feedback for scholars at all stages of development. The LatCrit leadership sought to gather and highlight much of this new scholarship in annual symposium volumes and other group publications (such as those in conjunction with South-North Exchange international conferences), many of which are discussed and cited in this Primer.

Early LatCrit participants, indeed, sought to shift what it meant to be a professional in the legal academy. Given the needs of our communities and existing structures of inequality, early LatCrit members had to assume an activist role. This embrace of a scholar-activist model meant subordinating the pursuit of promotions, titles, and career advancement to collective interests. A central strategy to sustain this activism was to redeploy the ample resources of the legal academy toward communal goals. For example, LatCrit carefully negotiated hotel contracts for annual conferences to ensure that a portion of participants' registration fees could support LatCrit's "portfolio of projects." LatCrit members, with sister organizations like SALT, also adopted "conferencing within conferences." This strategy allowed LatCrit members to more effectively manage limited conference travel budgets to facilitate multiple meetings per year, carving out time at larger annual conferences (including those sponsored by LatCrit, SALT, and the Association of American Law Schools) to pursue LatCrit collaborative projects. LatCrit also incorporated itself (a rare move for academic organizations of law faculty) in order to provide principled and professional stewardship of its financial resources.

These collectivist and transformational successes, however, always coexisted uneasily with a constant churn of members welcomed under LatCrit's "open door/big tent" disposition who came to a few conferences, published in a few symposia, and then departed with improved CVs. From the beginning, LatCrit struggled with the tensions created by its fundamental contradiction. The organization, and its individual members, were by the very nature of their political-economic position pushed and pulled between institutional norms: collectivism versus careerism; structural transformation versus "one-off" reforms; collaborative projects versus siloed projects; and effective stewardship versus hierarchy.

Contemporary Challenges: Darkness at the Edge of Town

As we go to publication in 2021, the political economy of U.S. academia has been utterly transformed from that of the 1990s. As neoliberalism took hold as the dominant mode of governance, it began to transform the economic conditions within which universities and law schools operated. Daniel Saunders summarizes the previous few decades in higher education:

As a part of the general reduction in funding social services and what were once considered public goods, public higher education has seen drastic cuts in state funding. The privatization and commercialization of previously publicly funded institutions extended to higher education, and as a result, these institutions became increasingly reliant on private funds. A substantial portion of those funds came from applied research that was financially supported and subsequently owned by private corporations. The role of the faculty and their institutional priorities were altered, with heavy emphasis placed on generating revenue and a lesser role in institutional decision-making. The tenure system, which neoliberals argued is economically irrational and a "bad investment" came under attack. Economic efficiency became a high priority for colleges and universities, which provided the rationale to use an unprecedented amount of part-time and adjunct faculty as well as to attack systems of shared governance. A college education was increasingly seen as a private good to be purchased by a student, who was redefined as a customer. Students, as rational economic actors, changed their goals from what were largely intrinsic, such as developing a meaningful philosophy of life, to larger extrinsic goals including being very well off financially. All of these are direct results of individuals and institutions using neoliberal policies and an economic rationality to make educational decisions, including attempts to treat and govern the university just like any traditional business, its faculty as traditional workers, and its students as customers.[8]

These structural and institutional changes were already well under way when the Great Recession of 2008 hit. The recession wrecked the business model of the largest, richest private law firms, as clients rebelled against the high fees and low transparency that the model represented.

Between 2008 and 2013, the top 250 private law firms lost more than 10,000 jobs, and some venerable law firms went under.[9] A new business model emerged, featuring a much smaller number of "superstar" partners with equity ownership and many more former partners demoted to employees; flatter fees, contingency and deferred fees, and "value billing" began to replace billable hours. This shock to the top tiers of the labor market ricocheted down through the entire structure and, ultimately, disrupted the law schools. Admissions went down, tuition went up, and student debt mounted. As one observer wrote in 2013: "The relationship among high tuition dependence, fewer high paying jobs, more moderate incomes, and the high debt load is creating the 'perfect storm' for many law students and, of course, now their law schools."[10]

And that was all before the pandemic of COVID-19.

Today, a sense of crisis is creating headwinds blowing against all transformative projects. The collapse of the law school business model and the ongoing crisis in higher education, combined with a sudden and dramatic loss of tuition revenues and uncertainty about when face-to-face education will be possible again, jeopardizes the very existence of some law schools and imposes shrinking budgets on all. Even for those schools not facing an existential crisis, the pandemic has intensified developments that jeopardize the financial model upon which LatCrit has traditionally relied: institution-funded, face-to-face meetings at conferences and workshops. These trends include the decimation or elimination of faculty travel budgets and summer research grants, in addition to the imposition of severe cuts to funds formerly subject to decanal discretion (reducing, for instance, the degree to which institutions will cosponsor LatCrit conferences). The pandemic has already forced many law schools to go entirely online, which sets up opportunities for a winner-take-all market in online teaching.[11]

The political environment accompanying this straitened economic environment may give the legal academy the postracial (and/or postpostracial), postintegration blues. At the admissions level, administrators engage in a desperate race for the right metrics in order to attract students: high LSAT scores (if the LSAT persists in these post–SAT/ACT days), high *US News and World Report* rankings, high bar-passage rates, and courses catered to producing "practice-ready" young lawyers. In the face of a national law school enrollment crisis, these administrators may be tempted to jettison student diversity as they chase high-LSAT applicants with ever-expanding "merit"-based scholarships and end up cannibalizing need-based and diversity-based scholarships.[12] Indeed, according to one study, disadvantaged law students already subsidize the attendance of their more privileged peers and graduate with disproportionately higher debt loads.[13]

At the hiring level, it is notable that, beginning around 2014, the Association of American Law Schools not only ceased providing public access to its annual *Statistical Report on Law Faculty* demographic survey but also refused to respond to numerous requests by scholars for explanation, retrieval, and/or reinstatement of this data.[14] As a result, the last year available for nationwide statistics on the racial and gender composition of law faculty is academic year 2008/09. What better way to acknowledge the postdiversity era than to stop taking account of racial data? One can further imagine hiring cutbacks, a return to the unicorn hiring model (via "rightsizing" the faculty or other reductions-in-force), and an intensification of anxious entitlement on the part of students burdened with debt, not sure what they are getting for their money in a partially or wholly virtual learning environment—all leading to the further ghettoization of CRT/LatCrit scholarship.

As a side note, in this moment of crisis we are seeing more women, and women of color, hired on as deans of law schools than ever before. In a move also seen in corporate America, women tend to be given the tiller in moments of institutional crisis when resources are at a minimum. We might call this the "Sinking ship? Put a woman in charge!" phenomenon. Given the precarity of contemporary legal education, however, this is an ironic achievement.

These developments across U.S. law schools at best destabilize the fundamental contradiction at the heart of LatCrit's mission; at worst, they threaten LatCrit's mission and membership. As we have seen, due to its structural position, LatCrit has always attracted some scholars committed to collective action and others primarily concerned with building a personal brand. If tenure-track positions become increasingly scarce, scholarship in general becomes devalued in contrast with teaching, and teaching becomes a student-pleasing, winner-take-all market, then it will be hard to interest junior faculty in transgressive scholarship. Instead, new faculty will be tempted to hunker down, conform, and attempt to ride out the storm alone rather than banding together to work for transformation. These pressures may produce a stark bifurcation between faculty hired in precrisis times, who may remain committed to LatCrit's transformative vision, and newer faculty, who see going along to get along as the only viable game in town.[15] In the new political economy of academia, LatCrit may find itself at odds with such institutionalized incentives, perhaps even eclipsed by people of color–led organizations whose mission is more explicitly careerist in the face of these pressures.

The Path Forward?

The challenge of the current moment is that the political-economic conditions in legal academia that made LatCrit possible seem no longer to be in place. Is it possible for LatCrit to overcome its fundamental contradiction—its commitment to radical projects whose successful execution depended on the financial health and largesse (or excesses) of the very institutions it was trying to transform? In light of the formidable shift in structural conditions, must LatCrit enter "survival mode"—exclusively virtual existence—and/or retreat into individual, albeit worthwhile, scholarly projects? Should LatCrit-affiliated faculty abandon building networks and focus on supporting their critically minded students and their local communities?

This "LatCrit-in-exile" future is certainly one possibility. However, we want to end where we began: by acknowledging the beauty, rage, and power of the Movement for Black Lives. In recent years we have seen uprisings not only by M4BL but also by youth demanding action in the face of climate change, in addition to an alliance of many groups who stood with the water protectors at Standing Rock to defy the Dakota Access Pipeline. This larger movement includes young (and experienced) lawyers and law students who challenged Donald Trump's racialized and inhumane immigration and asylum policies to render direct assistance in border towns, airports, and sanctuary cities.[16] It includes legal professionals marching alongside M4BL and working to deploy legal skills and knowledge to end institutionalized violence against Black people and transform institutions to promote Black flourishing.[17] Indeed, young lawyers are hard at work not only fighting the bad but also building the new—developing legal tools for sustainable and just economies, mutual aid in times of crisis, and security without a carceral state.[18] Given the multiple linked pandemics described in the foreword to this book, we need LatCrit's transformative spirit of resistance and disposition more than ever.

Sociologist Alondra Nelson, writing of Afrofuturism, notes that "dystopia can be an enduring state for Black communities, but . . . utopia is also always being imagined, embodied, dreamed, and constituted in everyday acts of thriving."[19] LatCrit represents that defiant spirit of resistance—*el espíritu de resistencia*—and foretells its persistence despite the odds. And perhaps, as Valdes and Bender have intimated in this Primer, the journey to freedom is just as important as the destination. We hope those who read this book will be inspired and moved to make new and better futures possible.

Sumi Cho is a founding member of LatCrit and recently retired from DePaul University College of Law.

Angela P. Harris is professor emerita at the University of California, Davis School of Law.

ACKNOWLEDGMENTS

We thank, first, the many and diverse pioneers whose work makes this book possible. Through this LatCrit book, or Primer, we recall, invoke, and celebrate them, while striving both to give back and to pay forward their efforts, gains, and goals. Toward that end, all author royalties from this publication are paid directly to the LatCrit nonprofit community treasury to sustain collective projects and the community itself. Thinking of future generations, we hope and ask that community members similarly keep community interests in mind and foster them whenever possible. Together, we can contribute to the ongoing and upcoming struggles of subordinated groups for equal justice, both within the academy and throughout society.

Early renditions of this Primer were spearheaded by such community and board members as Roberto Corrada, Charles Venator-Santiago, and Pedro Malavet during the 1990s, for which we are very grateful. Laura E. Gómez aided the development of the book by assigning an early draft to her Advanced Critical Race Theory students at UCLA for their helpful feedback. Additionally, we are specifically grateful to Margaret Montoya, Angela Harris, Sumi Cho, and Tayyab Mahmud for their individual contributions to, and support of, this publication. We appreciate equally the time, encouragement, and support of our law deans, Tony Varona and Annette Clark, and the hard work of our research assistant on the afterword, Ariana Headrick, our administrative assistants Marysabel Merino and Laurie Wells, and Seattle law librarian Kerry Fitz-Gerald. As authors, we own all errors and shortcomings.

REPRINT CREDITS—Portions of select published LatCrit symposia were reworked or quoted in the text, as credited in the above text. For

those permissions we are grateful to the individual authors of Angela
Harris, Berta Esperanza Hernández-Truyol, and Margaret Montoya,
and to the following law reviews: *UCLA Chicano-Latino Law Review*
(for Berta Hernandez-Truyol, Angela P. Harris & Francisco Valdes,
*Afterword—Beyond the First Decade: A Forward-Looking History of Lat-
Crit Theory, Community and Praxis*, 26 CHICANO-LATINO L. REV.
237 (2006)), the *Seattle Journal for Social Justice* (for Steven Bender &
Francisco Valdes, with Shelley Cavalieri, Jasmine Gonzalez Rose, Saru
Matambanadzo, Roberto Corrada, Jorge Roig, Tayyab Mahmud, Zsea
Bowmani & Anthony E. Varona, *Afterword—What's Next? Into a Third
Decade of LatCrit Theory, Community, and Praxis*, 16 SEATTLE J. SOC.
JUST. 823 (2018) (reprinted with the permission of the Seattle Journal
for Social Justice)), the *FIU Law Review* (for Margaret E. Montoya and
Francisco Valdes, *Afterword—"Latinas/os" and Latina/o Legal Studies:
A Critical and Self-Critical Review of LatCrit Theory and Legal Models
of Knowledge Production*, 4 FIU L. REV. 187 (2008)), and the *Journal
of Race, Gender, and Poverty* (for Francisco Valdes, *Afterword: Theory
Without Borders: LatCritical Approaches to South-North Legal Frame-
works and Hemispheric Justice Studies*, 5 J. RACE, GENDER & POV-
ERTY 1 (No. 2, 2013–14)).

PHOTO CREDITS—Longtime LatCrit community member Tayyab
Mahmud, Seattle University School of Law, supplied the photographs
throughout this book, with the exception of the SNX Antigua photo in
chapter 5 taken by an unknown community member.

GENERAL DISCUSSION QUESTIONS

These questions connect to the above account of LatCrit theory, com-munity, and praxis and are supplied for both classroom use and self-reflection about academic activism in the form of LatCrit and beyond.

What are some of the pressures, incentives, or interests at play in sti-fling progressive academic activism?

What is LatCrit's model/strategy/blueprint to blunt or overcome those interests and pressures?

What are some of the key scholarly contributions of LatCrit? How do they, or can they, connect to actions or practice toward a postsubordina-tion future?

What are the metrics you (or LatCrit as an organization) might use to judge the "success" of LatCrit's academic activism?

Should law professors engage in academic activism? Is all legal (and other) scholarship in some way political?

What can we learn from struggles in other places when struggle exists and is needed in our own "backyard?"

As LatCrit aims to develop a critical, activist, and interdisciplinary dis-course on law and society affecting Latinas/os/x who were being ignored for the most part in prior discourses, should it have taken steps to limit its membership and participation to Latinas/os/x?

This Primer describes the attributes of the so-called critical classroom. Do (or did) those mirror your educational experience in law school or another educational setting? If not, what is/was missing?

What were your reactions to this Primer? Did anything seem missing? Did anything in particular resonate with you?

How can "theory" contribute to local and global struggles against subordination?

What do you see as the necessary ingredients, conditions, or circumstances to foment social change toward a postsubordination future?

What role can students play in LatCrit and other critical/activist social movements steeped in the development of outsider jurisprudence?

APPENDIX A

LatCrit Self-Study

I. LATCRIT SELF-STUDY PROCESS: LATCRIT XIII (2008)–LATCRIT
XIV (2009)

- FALL 2008: The Annual Board Meeting (ABM) at LatCrit XIII in Seattle
  during October 2008 focuses on internal self-governance structures and
  intergenerational transitions, including issues related to strategic planning;
  to follow up, the Steering Committee organizes a special Board meeting in
  Denver, CO during December 2008, which results in creation of the Lat-
  Crit Self-Study Task Force to conduct a substantive review of our internal
  status quo and produce recommendations.
- SPRING 2009: Board meets at AALS in San Diego during January 2009
  and ratifies creation and funding of the Self-Study Task Force, which develops and administers a Board-wide survey and interview process, including
  in-person interviews during March 2009 at the CRT20 Conference in Iowa
  City, IA and at the South-North Exchange (SNX) in Santiago de Chile during May.
- SUMMER 2009: Task Force meets in Miami, FL during July 2009 to
  compile its findings into the LatCrit Evolution Task Force Report and
  Recommendations and presents it to the Board, first by email, and later at a
  special Board meeting in Seattle, WA during August 2009, for preliminary
  review, feedback, and discussion.
- FALL 2009: Board approves for implementation many of the Task Force
  recommendations at the ABM at LatCrit XIV in Washington, D.C., during October 2009; Board appoints a Transition Team to revise the Bylaws
  accordingly and identify other necessary follow-up steps. To conclude
  and memorialize the Self-Study process, the Task Force Report and

Recommendations are featured and discussed in both the LatCrit XIII and LatCrit XIV symposia Afterwords.

II. STRATEGIC PLANNING PROCESS: LATCRIT XIV (2009)–LATCRIT XVI (2011)

- FALL 2009: Transition Team revises the LatCrit Bylaws to reflect Board adoption of Self-Study recommendations at LatCrit XIV ABM in Washington, D.C., during October 2009.
- SPRING 2010: Board meets at AALS in New Orleans, LA during January 2010 to consider and approve Bylaw revisions; Steering Committee meets in Los Angeles, CA after the UCLA Critical Race Studies Conference during March 2010 to outline remaining programmatic and institutional issues for substantive discussions and Board decisions in strategic planning process.
- SUMMER 2010: Board Retreat convenes in Mexico City, Mexico, after SNX during May 2010 to consider and develop the Steering Committee's outline of issues.
- FALL 2010: Steering Committee develops Report and Recommendations based on Board Retreat for presentation to Board at LatCrit XV ABM in Denver, CO during October 2010; Board partially adopts them while deferring action on the remainder until the Board meeting at the AALS in San Francisco, CA during January 2011.
- SPRING 2011: Board declines to act on remaining parts of Steering Committee Report and Recommendations during its meeting at the AALS in San Francisco, CA during January 2011, calling instead for further study, reflection, and discussion.
- SUMMER 2011: Steering Committee Retreat convenes in Miami, FL during July 2011 to develop further recommendations for presentation to Board at LatCrit XVI ABM in San Diego, CA.
- FALL 2011: Board meets in San Diego, CA at LatCrit XVI ABM during October 2011 to consider and act upon Steering Committee's follow-up work and conclude the Strategic Planning process.

APPENDIX B

LatCrit Annual/Biennial Conference Publications, 1996–2020

1. *Founding Colloquium*: Dorado, Puerto Rico, Oct. 13–14, 1995; Colloquium, *Representing Latina/o Communities: Critical Race Theory and Practice*, 9 BERKELEY LA RAZA L.J. 1 (1996) (known as "LatCrit ½").

2. *LatCrit I*: La Jolla, California, May 2–5, 1996; Symposium, *LatCrit Theory: Naming and Launching a New Discourse of Critical Legal Scholarship*, 2 HARV. LATINO L. REV. 1 (1997).

3. *LatCrit II*: San Antonio, Texas, May 1–4, 1997; Symposium, *Difference, Solidarity and Law: Building Latina/o Communities through LatCrit Theory*, 19 CHICANO-LATINO L. REV. 1 (1998).

4. *LatCrit III*: Miami, Florida, May 7–10, 1998; Symposium, *Comparative Latinas/os: Identity, Law and Policy in LatCrit Theory*, 53 U. MIAMI L. REV. 575 (1999).

5. *LatCrit IV*: Lake Tahoe, California April 29–May 2, 1999; Symposium, *Rotating Centers, Expanding Frontiers: LatCrit Theory and Marginal Intersections*, 33 U.C. DAVIS L. REV. 751 (2000).

6. *LatCrit V*: Breckenridge, Colorado, May 4–7, 2000; Symposium, *Class in LatCrit: Theory and Praxis in a World of Economic Inequality*, 78 DENVER U. L. REV. 467 (2001).

7. *LatCrit VI*: Gainesville, Florida, April 26–29, 2001; Symposium, *Latinas/os and the Americas: Centering North-South Frameworks in LatCrit Theory*, 55 U. FLA. L. REV. 1 (2003) and 54 RUTGERS L. REV. 803 (2002).

8. *LatCrit VII*: Portland, Oregon, May 2–5, 2002; Symposium, *Coalitional Theory and Praxis: Social Movements and LatCrit Community*, 81 OR. L. REV. 587 (2002), and 13 LA RAZA L.J. 113 (2002).

9. *LatCrit VIII*: Cleveland, Ohio, May 1–4, 2003; Symposium, *City and Citizen: Operations of Power, Strategies of Resistance*, 52 CLEV. ST. L. REV. 1 (2005).

10. *LatCrit IX*: Malvern, Pennsylvania, April 29–May 1, 2004; Symposium, *Countering Kulturkampf Politics through Critique and Justice Pedagogy*, 50 VILL. L. REV. 4 (2005), 35 SETON HALL L. REV. 1155 (2005).

11. *LatCrit X*: San Juan, Puerto Rico October 6–10, 2005; Symposium, *Critical Approaches to Economic In/Justice: LatCrit at Ten Years*, 26 CHICANO-LATINO L. REV. 1 (2006) and 17 LA RAZA L.J. 1 (2006).

12. *LatCrit XI:* Las Vegas, Nevada, October 5–8, 2006; Symposium, *Working and Living in the Global Playground: Frontstage and Backstage,* 7 NEV. L.J. 685 (2007).

13. *LatCrit XII:* Miami, Florida, October 4–6, 2007; Symposium, *Critical Localities: Epistemic Communities, Rooted Cosmopolitans, New Hegemonies and Knowledge Processes,* 4 FLA. INT'L U. L. REV. 1 (2008).

14. *LatCrit XIII:* Seattle, Washington, October 2–4, 2008; Symposium, *Representation and Republican Governance: Critical Interrogation of Electoral Systems and the Exercise of the Franchise,* 8 SEATTLE J. SOC. JUST. 1 (2009).

15. *LatCrit XIV:* Bethesda, Maryland, October 1–4, 2009; Symposium, *Outsiders Inside: Critical Outsiders Theory and Praxis in the Policymaking of the New American Regime,* 18 AM. U. J. GENDER SOC. POL'Y & L. 367 (2010).

16. *LatCrit XV:* Denver, Colorado, October 7–10, 2010; Symposium, *The Color of the Economic Crisis: Exploring the Downturn from the Bottom Up,* 14 HARV. LATINO L. REV. 243 (2011), 1 U. MIAMI RACE & SOC. JUST. L. REV. 1 (2011), and 22 LA RAZA L.J. 1 (2012).

17. *LatCrit XVI:* San Diego, California, October 6–9, 2011; Symposium, *Global Justice: Theories, Histories, Futures,* 48 CAL. W. L. REV. 231 (2012) and 42 CAL. W. INT'L L.J. 265 (2012).

18. *LatCrit 2013: First Biennial Conference:* Chicago, Illinois, October 3–6, 2013; Symposium, *Resistance Rising: Theorizing and Building Cross-Sector Movements,* 12 SEATTLE J. SOC. JUST. 699 (2014) and 47 J. MARSHALL L. REV. 1181 (2014).

19. *LatCrit 2015: Twentieth Anniversary Conference:* Anaheim, California, October 1–3, 2015; Symposium, *Critical Constitutionalism: Social Justice Change and Outsider Legal Studies,* 37 WHITTIER L. REV. 335 (2016) and 10 CHARLESTON L. REV. 173 (2016).

20. *LatCrit 2017:* Orlando, Florida, September 29–30, 2017; Symposium, *What's Next? Resistance Resilience and Community in the Trump Era,* 9 U. MIAMI RACE & SOC. JUST. L. REV. 1 (2019), and 16 SEATTLE J. SOC. JUST. 607 (2018).

21. *LatCrit 2019:* Atlanta, Georgia, October 18–19, 2019; Symposium, *The Dispossessed Majority: Resisting the Second Redemption in América Postfascista (Postfascist America),* 23 HARV. LATINX L. REV. 149 (2020) and forthcoming LA RAZA L.J.

APPENDIX C

International and Comparative Law Colloquium Publications, 1996–2020

1. International Law, Human Rights and LatCrit Theory, Miami, Florida, 1996; Colloquium, *International Law, Human Rights and LatCrit Theory*, 28 U. MIAMI INTER-AM. L. REV. 177 (1997).

2. Human Rights Law and LatCrit Theory After *Pinochet*, Malaga, Spain, 1999; Colloquium, *Spain, the Americas, Latino/as: International and Comparative Law in Triangular Perspective*, 9 U. MIAMI INT'L. & COMP. L. REV. 1 (2000) (publishing the proceedings of the second and third ICCs, held during 1998 and 1999 in Malaga, Spain).

3. The Power to Order: Placing the Legal Control of Sexualities in Comparative and International Perspective, Malaga, Spain, 2000; Colloquium, *Spain, the Americas, Latino/as: International and Comparative Law in Triangular Perspective*, 9 U. MIAMI INT'L. & COMP. L. REV.1 (2000) (publishing the proceedings of the second and third ICCs, held during 1998 and 1999 in Malaga, Spain).

4. Colonialism, Globalization and Law, Buenos Aires, Argentina, 2003; Colloquium, *LatCrit Theory and Inter-American Studies: South-North Perspectives*, 38 REV. JURÍDICA U. INTER. P.R 1 (2003) (ICC IV).

5. LatCrit Theory and Praxis in International Contexts, Cape Town, South Africa, 2004; Colloquium, *Centering Constitutionalism: LatCritical Theory in International and Comparative Law*, 14 GRIFFITH U.L. REV. 143 (2005).

6. Globalizing Equality Theory, Constructing Material Justice: The Next Critical Project, Paris, France, 2010; Symposium, *The Color of the Economic Crisis: Exploring the Downturn from the Bottom Up*, 22 LA RAZA L.J. 1 (2012) (ICC papers published as part of the LatCrit XV Symposium).

APPENDIX D

South-North Exchange Publications, 2003–2020

1. Beyond Formal Democracy: Re-conceiving Self Determination, San Juan, Puerto Rico, 2003; Colloquium, *Law, Culture, and Society: LatCrit Theory and Transdisciplinary Approaches to Law and Policy*, 16 Fla. J. Int'l L. 539 (2004).

2. Reconstituting Constitutions and Cultures: Neoliberalism, Social Justice and the Rule of Law, San Juan, Puerto Rico, 2004; Symposium, *Law, Culture and Indigenous People: Comparative and Critical Perspectives*, 17 Fla. J. Int'l L. 449 (2005) (publishing the proceedings of the second and third SNX).

3. The Americas and Their Indigenous People: Assessing the International Decade of the World's Indigenous People (1994–2004), San Juan, Puerto Rico, 2005; Symposium, *Law, Culture and Indigenous People: Comparative and Critical Perspectives*, 17 Fla. J. Int'l L. 449 (2005) (publishing the proceedings of the second and third SNX).

4. Bogotá, Colombia, 2006; Symposium, *Free Market Fundamentalism: A Critical Review of Dogmas and Consequences*, 5 Seattle J. Soc. Just. 497 (2007).

5. Rio De Janeiro, Brazil, 2007; Symposium, *Race and Color Across the Americas: Comparative Constructions of Racial and Ethnic Subjugation*, 21 Nat'l Black L.J 1 (2009).

6. Santiago, Chile, 2009; Symposium, *Legal/Political Progressivism and Public Policies in the Americas*, Pace Int'l L. Rev. (Online Companion) 1 (2010).

7. Mexico City, Mexico, 2010; Symposium, *The Global Politics of Food: Sustainability and Subordination*, 43 U. Miami Inter-Am. L. Rev. 1 (2011).

8. Santo Domingo, Dominican Republic, 2011; Symposium, *Migratory Currents in the Americas*, Corrientes Migratorias en las Americas, 46 Rev. Jurídica U. Inter. P.R 723 (2011–2012).

9. Curridabat, Costa Rica, 2012; Symposium, *The Changing Face of Justice: Access to the Inter-American System of Human Rights*, 3 Creighton Int'l & Comp. L.J. 128 (2013).

10. San Juan, Puerto Rico, 2013; Symposium, *The Costs of Exclusion: Austerity Policies and Anti-Social Governmental Strategies*, 5 J. Race, Gender & Poverty 1 (No. 2, 2013–14).

11. Towards an Education for Justice: South-North Perspectives, Bogotá, Colombia, 2014; Symposium, *Challenges to Justice Education: South-North Perspectives*, 9 Charleston L. Rev. 213 (2015).

12. Leading from the South: Politics of Gender, Sex and Sexualities, Santo Domingo, Dominican Republic, 2016 (no publication).

13. From Extraction to Emancipation: Development Reimagined, Antigua, Guatemala, 2018; Symposium (untitled), 25 U.C. DAVIS J. INT'L L. & POL'Y 1 (Fall 2018 and Spring 2019).

APPENDIX E

Study Space Publications, 2007–2020

1. Entering the 21st Century: Challenges and Opportunities of Panama's Explosive Urban Growth, Panama City, Panama, 2007; Symposium, *Panama's Explosive Urban Growth*, 4 TENN. J. L. & POL'Y 158 (2008).
2. Bogotá, Colombia, 2008; Symposium, *Multicultural Colombia: Urban & Rural Lands, Rights of Self-Governance and Cultural Difference*, 40 U. MIAMI INTER-AM. L. REV. 197 (2009).
3. Social and Cultural Demands on Private and Public Lands in the Post-Colonial North American West: Managing the "City Beautiful," Denver, Colorado, 2008 (papers published as part of the LatCrit 2013 Conference Symposium); Symposium, *Resistance Rising: Theorizing and Building Cross-Sector Movements*, 12 SEATTLE J. SOC. JUST. 913 (2014).
4. The Use and Control of Space and Institutions for Social Transformation—the Case of Medellín, Medellín, Colombia, 2009; Symposium, *Multicultural Colombia: Urban & Rural Lands, Rights of Self-Governance and Cultural Difference*, 41 U. MIAMI INTER-AM. L. REV. 1 (2009).
5. Rio de Janeiro, Brazil, 2010; Symposium, *Inclusive and Sustainable Rio: Cultural Diversity, Property and the Environment*, 44 U. MIAMI INTER-AM. L. REV. 139 (2013).
6. Comparative Systems in Law and Society, Havana, Cuba, 2013 (no publication).
7. Corporations, the State, and the Rule of Law, Guatemala, 2015; published book FROM EXTRACTION TO EMANCIPATION: REIMAGINING DEVELOPMENT FOR GUATEMALA (Carolina Academic Press and ABA Section of International Law 2017).

APPENDIX F

Free-standing Symposium Publications and Books

SYMPOSIA

1. Symposium—*LatCrit: Latinas/os and the Law*, 85 CAL. L. REV. 1087 (1997), 10 LA RAZA L.J. 1 (1998).
2. Symposium—*Culture, Language, Sexuality and Law: LatCrit Theory and the Construction of the Nation*, 5 MICH. J. RACE & L. 787 (2000), 33 U. MICH. J. L. REFORM 203 (2000).
3. Symposium—*LatCrit Praxis @ XX: Toward Equal Justice in Law, Education and Society*, 90 CHI.-KENT L. REV. 361 (2015).

BOOKS

1. FROM EXTRACTION TO EMANCIPATION: REIMAGINING DEVELOPMENT FOR GUATEMALA (Carolina Academic Press and ABA Section of International Law 2017).
2. CRITICAL JUSTICE: SYSTEMIC ADVOCACY IN LAW AND SOCIETY (West Academic 2021).

LatCrit Scholarship Research Toolkit Thematic Index—List of Themes

1 Critical Outsider Jurisprudence/Legal Philosophy
2 Religion & Churches
3 Race, Ethnicities, Nationalities, & Colors
4 Class & Identity
5 Critical Coalitions & Social Transformations
6 Languages, Cultures & Families
7 Sexes & Genders
8 Sexual Orientations and Gender Identities
9 Indigenous Peoples & LatCrit Theory
10 Asians & Latinas/os/x
11 Popular Culture & LatCrit Theory
12 Mass Communication & Mass Control
13 International and Hemispheric Law, Human Rights
14 Globalization, Economic Integration
15 Conquests, Migrations & Diasporas, Immigration
16 Legal Systems
17 Democracy, Governance & Self Determination
18 Comparativism In & Through LatCrit Theory
19 Labor & Employment
20 Security, Terror & Borders
21 Education & Legal Knowledge
22 Land Policy & Social Justice
23 Food, Healthcare & Well-being
24 Environmental In/Justice
25 Crime & Punishment

APPENDIX H

Excerpt from Mission Statement for Living Justice Institute at Campo Sano

[Campo Sano offers] a safe, peaceful haven for the cultivation of critical communities and coalitions based on shared social justice commitments. Among these, specifically, are the substantive values, functions, guideposts and postulates formulated by LatCrit, RaceCrit, FemCrit, QueerCrit, ClassCrit and other OutCrit scholars and activists since the late twentieth century. Through the work of the LJI and affiliated persons or partners, Campo Sano now provides a self-sustaining and self-directed sanctuary to incubate decolonizing knowledge and consciousness, foster egalitarian human society, and engender activist academic democracy for generations to come.

Broadly speaking, we hope and intend that the LJI at Campo Sano proactively will plan, host, facilitate and sponsor programs and projects of all kinds consistent with the LatCrit Charter and Bylaws, including, but not limited to, projects and programs designed to inspire and develop:

- LatCrit theory, community and praxis in every respect;
- Pipelines, communities, networks and coalitions consistent with LatCrit theory, community and praxis;
- Educational initiatives to promote public understanding and social correction of human and environmental injustice, and related issues of equality, dignity and freedom both in the U.S. and internationally;
- Constitutional, legal and policy frameworks for the protection of equal justice for all, and civil/human rights generally, toward the establishment of an open, post-subordination, egalitarian U.S. and global society;

- Transnational, transcultural and transdisciplinary discourses, knowledges, activities and alliances toward the establishment of global equal justice across Earth;
- Publications and other kinds of informational resources of any kind, both electronic and traditional, consistent with LatCrit principles and practices and critical outsider jurisprudence; [and]
- Intentional communities and other kinds of justice-centered groups, organizations, entities or formations of any sort committed to living justice in every respect and in principled, enduring terms.

NOTES

FOREWORD: THE *GRAN TRECHO* THAT IS LATCRIT

My father, Ricardo Montoya, was fond of Spanish *dichos* (wise sayings or proverbs), and one of his favorites was "*Del dicho al hecho hay gran trecho*," which means that there is a long distance between promising something and actually getting it done—"*trecho*" is the distance between two points. Those of us who met in the early years, before we were known as LatCrit, could wish that we would extend collectively well into a second decade and beyond, but we couldn't know that the journey would cover a very long distance, *un gran trecho*.

This essay is dedicated to my daughters, Diana and Alejandra, *quienes son mis tesoros, mi orgullo, y el motivo por mis esfuerzos.* My gratitude goes to my husband, my daughters, and my friends Sumi Cho and Verónica Gonzales-Zamora, who read my drafts, honed my thinking, and sharpened the analysis.

Epigraph: *See Malcolm X Quotes and the Story of His Life, Wife, and Children.* ANSWERS AFRICA, https://answersafrica.com/by-these-quotes-you-know-malcom-x.html. Note: The provenance of this quote remains in question, but it is widely attributed to Malcolm X.

1   *See* Gustavo López and Ana Gonzalez-Barrera, *Afro-Latino: A Deeply Rooted Identity among U.S. Hispanics,* PEW RESEARCH CENTER, Mar. 1, 2016, www.pewresearch.org/fact-tank/2016/03/01/afro-latino-a-deeply-rooted-identity-among-u-s-hispanics.

2   *See* Jorge Ramos, *A Hard Conversation for the Latino Community,* N.Y. TIMES, July 3, 2020, www.nytimes.com/2020/07/03/opinion/ramos-afro-latinos-racism .html?smid=nytcore-ios-share.

3   *See* Miguel Salazar, *The Problem with Latinidad,* THE NATION, Sept. 16, 2019, www.thenation.com/article/archive/hispanic-heritage-month-latinidad.

4   *See* Kurly Tlapoyawa, *What "Latinx" Doesn't Include,* YES!, Nov. 22, 2019, www .yesmagazine.org/opinion/2019/11/22/latinx-indigenous-history-heritage.

5   *See Missing and Murdered Indigenous Womxn, Girls, and Two Spirit,* COALITION TO STOP VIOLENCE AGAINST NATIVE WOMEN, 2020, www.csvanw.org/mmiw.

6   *See* Margaret E. Montoya, Máscaras, Trenzas y Greñas: *Un/Masking the Self While Un/Braiding Latina Stories and Legal Discourse,* 17 HARV. WOMEN'S L.J. 185 (1994) (*concurrently published in* 15 CHICANO-LATINO L. REV. 1 (1994)).

7   *See* Amanda Lanthorne, *Historical Note: Chicana and Chicano Studies Department* (1969–), https://scua2.sdsu.edu/archon/?p=creators/creator&id=259#:~:text=Hist orical%20Note%3A,a%20major%20and%20a%20minor.

8   *See* Two videos showing the BLM protests in all fifty states, https://www.facebook. com/quianna.chaney/videos/10112774424443045/ and www.youtube.com/ watch?v=SG4LiBwtWCY.

9   *See WHO Coronavirus Disease (COVID-19) Dashboard,* WORLD HEALTH ORGANIZATION, Nov. 20, 2020, https://covid19.who.int.

10 *See The COVID Tracking Project,* THE ATLANTIC MONTHLY GROUPS, CovidTracking.com. 2020, https://covidtracking.com/race.

11 *Ibid.* (counties with the twenty highest death rates).

12 See Morbidity and Mortality Weekly Report, Race, Ethnicity, and Age Trends in Persons Who Died from COVID-19—United States, May–August 2020, CENTERS FOR DISEASE CONTROL AND PREVENTION, www.cdc.gov/mmwr/volumes /69/wr/mm6942e1.htm.

13 *Ibid.*

14 *Ibid.*

15 *See New Medicine for the Inequalities That Are Making Us Sick,* STRUCTURAL COMPETENCY, https://structuralcompetency.org/about-2.

16 *See* Paul Davidson, *1.5M More Workers File for Unemployment Even as Many Americans Return to Work Amid COVID-19,* USA TODAY, June 11, 2020, www .usatoday.com/story/money/2020/06/11/jobless-claims-report-another-million -file-unemployment-coronavirus/5338163002.

17 *See U6 Unemployment Trends,* www.macrotrends.net/1377/u6-unemployment-rate#:~:text=U3%20is%20the%20official%20unemployment,of%20May%20 2020%20is%2021.20.

18 See Weekly Unemployment Claims Dip Slightly in Last Report Before Election, WASHINGTON POST, Oct. 29, 2020, www.washingtonpost.com/business/2020/10 /29/october-unemployment-claims-election.

19   *See Total Unemployed, Plus All Persons Marginally Attached to the Labor Force, Plus Total Employed Part Time for Economic Reasons, as a Percent of the Civilian Labor Force Plus All Persons Marginally Attached to the Labor Force (U-6),* FEDERAL RESERVE BANK OF ST. LOUIS, ECONOMIC RESEARCH, Oct. 1, 2020, https://fred.stlouisfed.org/series/U6RATE.

20 *See Local Governments Continue to Lose Non-education Related Jobs, Despite Continued Recovery of Other Major Sectors,* NATIONAL ASSOCIATION OF COUNTIES, July 2, 2020, www.naco.org/covid19/topic/research-data/june -jobs-report.

21 *See Unemployment Level-Permanent Job Losers,* FEDERAL RESERVE BANK OF ST. LOUIS, ECONOMIC RESEARCH, Sept. 2020, https://fred.stlouisfed.org /series/lns13026638.

22 *See* Jim Tankersley & Emily Cochrane, *Congress Eyes More Spending as Virus Surges and Economy Struggles,* N.Y. TIMES, July 2, 2020, www.nytimes. com/2020/07/02/business/economy/congress-economy-coronavirus.html.

23 See *Biden Calls for Congress To Pass Another Coronavirus Relief Package. But There's No Sign of a Stimulus Deal as Holidays Approach*, CNBC, Nov. 17, 2020, www.cnbc.com/2020/11/17/biden-calls-for-coronavirus-stimulus-but-theres-no -sign-of-a-deal.html.

24 See *In Letter to Congress: Black Wealth 2020 Sends Plea for Unity in Pandemic Relief*, CHARLESTON CHRONICLE, May 27, 2020, www.charlestonchronicle. net/2020/05/27/in-letter-to-congress-black-wealth-2020-sends-plea-for-unity-in -pandemic-relief.

25 See Beth Gardiner, *Unequal Impact: The Deep Links Between Racism and Climate Change*, YALE ENVIRONMENT 360, June 9, 2020, https://e360.yale.edu/features /unequal-impact-the-deep-links-between-inequality-and-climate-change.

26 *Ibid.*

PREFACE

Epigraph: Sumi K. Cho, *Essential Politics*, 2 HARV. LATINO L. REV. 433, 441, 444, 455 (1997).

1. BACKGROUND AND ORIGINS

Epigraph: Margaret Montoya, *Foreword—LatCrit at Ten Years*, 26 CHICANA /O- LATINA/O L. REV. 1–14, 13 (2006).

1 Margaret E. Montoya & Francisco Valdes, *Afterword—"Latinas/os" and Latina/o Legal Studies: A Critical and Self-Critical Review of LatCrit Theory and Legal Models of Knowledge Production*, 4 FIU L. REV. 187 (2008). It bears emphasis that LatCrit theory—like outsider jurisprudence generally—emerged during times of backlash and retrenchment, including opposition to affirmative action values as well as hostility to critical studies and scholars within the legal academy. *See, e.g.*, Richard M. Fischl, *The Question That Killed Critical Legal Studies*, 17 LAW & SOC. INQUIRY 779 (1992) (discussing the backlash campaign against the Crits and why/how it succeeded); Margaret E. Montoya, *A Brief History of Chicana/o School Segregation: One Rationale for Affirmative Action*, 12 LA RAZA L.J. 159 (2002); Margaret E. Montoya, *Of "Subtle Prejudices," White Supremacy, and Affirmative Action: A Reply to Paul Butler*, 68 U. COLO. L. REV. 891 (1997) (a colloquy on applying affirmative action jurisprudence to criminal- ization and incarceration practices); Symposium, *Countering Kulturkampf Through Critique and Justice Pedagogy*, 50 VILL. L. REV. 749 (2005) (publishing some of the papers presented to the Ninth Annual LatCrit Conference, focused generally on this phenomenon). As these varied sources indicate, this academic backlash is part and parcel of the larger "culture wars" aimed at reversing New Deal, Civil Rights, and Great Society lawmaking legacies. *See generally infra* note 18, chapter 4 and sources cited therein on the US culture wars.

2 *See* chapter 2 for discussion of the antisubordination principle/value.

3 As much of the LatCrit literature demonstrates, early on (since the mid-1990s)
   we chose to describe this identity as "Latina/o" in order to include an emphasis on
   women and invert the familiar masculine phrasing. A review of our website
   materials manifests the point. www.latcrit.org. Using Latina/o, as opposed to
   Hispanic, or "his panic," offered the linguistic possibility to feature the female
   gender. We acknowledge and commend the current debate over Latinx as a more
   inclusive way to denote "Latin"-origin persons or populations beyond traditional
   linguistic gendering. For purposes of this Primer, which details the LatCrit
   experience thus far, we use the Latina/o reference when that reference was used in
   text being quoted, as in article or conference panel titles, while using the
   Latina/o/x reference for any new text. Some of those titles cited may alternatively
   refer to just Latinas or just Latinos, or a few to Latino/a. Although the "LatCrit"
   name is somewhat positioned to encompass the societal evolution of referencing
   Latin-origin persons, the organization's formal, incorporated name was a product
   of the early LatCrit community decision to invert the masculine phrasing and
   emphasize women—Latina and Latino Critical Legal Theory, Inc., a Florida
   nonprofit corporation. We have not yet had a community conversation around
   changing the organizational name, nor an accounting of the intellectual (and
   physical) property LatCrit has acquired or registered in its current name and how
   those ownerships could be adjusted, and the attendant expense of that. Those
   conversations may come, and we invite them, while ever mindful from past
   community scholarship that both Latin(a/o/x) and Hispanic-derived references
   nonetheless replicate colonized legacies. See Luz Guerra, *LatCrit Y La Des-
   Colonización Nuestra: Taking Colón Out*, 19 CHICANO-LATINO L. REV. 351,
   355 (1998):
   > This juncture has critical implications for Latinos, for what some call
   > "outsider discourse" and "critical race theory," as well as for legal
   > scholarship—beginning with a name which may or may not be the name
   > we would have chosen for ourselves, depending on which parallel reality
   > you occupy. Before [Cristóbal] Colón [known also as Christopher
   > Columbus] we were many. We were not Americans. We were not hyphen-
   > ated. "Hispanic" came with Colón. "Latino" came with Colón. Since Colón,
   > one common experience has been trying to "de-colón," decolonize, take
   > Colón out.
   > At the same time, we recognize that an institutional name is mostly free of
   > gender-bound legal restrictions on individual residents in many jurisdictions
   > that may prevent changes sought by those individuals to better capture one's
   > gender for official identity purposes.
   > With regard to both LatCrit as a shorthand designation, and the institutional
   > name of Latina and Latino Critical Legal Theory, Inc., we further recognize that
   > Latina/Latino/Latinx as terminology does not always travel outside the United
   > States and means something different within the U.S. racial cosmology than in

some Latin American countries. The naming of the LatCrit organization, based
on the term Latina/o, came from an almost exclusively U.S. academic group early
on at its mid-1990s origin. The "Lat" reflects our choice within that situatedness
in favor of Latina/o (rather than Hispanic—the alternative at that time) both to
counter the gendering of the language as well as to identify with the darker-
skinned "bottom" of these groups or communities (because "Hispanic" is used in
these communities as a way of asserting and signaling racial superiority—a claim
of whiteness based on Spanish race systems).

4 "LatCrit" theory is a jurisprudential subject position that encompasses richly
diverse scholars and texts. "LatCrit theory" comprises many scholars with varying
views, making it somewhat misleading to speak of LatCrit theory in the singular.
Nonetheless, the diverse range of critical legal scholars who have coalesced
around the collective effort to articulate LatCrit theory have "exhibited . . . [a]
sense of shared groupness." *See* Francisco Valdes, *Foreword—Latina/o Ethnicities,
Critical Race Theory, and Post-Identity Politics In Postmodern Legal Culture: From
Practices To Possibilities,* 9 L A R A Z A L.J. 1, 7, n.25 (1996). LatCrit members, like
"Latinas/os/x" and other social groups, are a collection of "different" individuals.
See Sylvia A. Marotta & Jorge G. Garcia, *Latinos in the United States in 2000,* 25
H I S P A N I C J. O F B E H A. S C I. 13 (2003); *see generally* T H E L A T I N O / A
C O N D I T I O N: A C R I T I C A L R E A D E R (Richard Delgado & Jean Stefancic eds.
1998). From the very beginning, LatCrit scholars have grappled with racial,
ethnic, and other forms of "diversity" both within and beyond "Latina/o/x"
communities.

5 The term "LatCrit" was coined at a 1995 colloquium, held in Puerto Rico, on the
relationship of critical race theory to "Latina/o" communities. From that
colloquium, the annual LatCrit conferences and other projects then flowed.
Information on LatCrit theory, including the full text of the inaugural LatCrit
symposium based on the LatCrit I Conference, can be obtained at the LatCrit
website, www.latcrit.org; *see also* Elizabeth M. Iglesias & Francisco Valdes,
*Afterword—Religion, Gender, Sexuality, Race and Class in Coalitional Theory: A
Critical and Self-Critical Analysis of LatCrit Social Justice Agendas,* 19 C H I C A N O -
L A T I N O L. R E V. 503, 568–71 (1998) (discussing the choice of "LatCrit" as partly a
political decision to identify as much as possible with people of color, Indigenous
people, and other traditionally subordinated groups in the construction of this
new discourse and praxis). The term "outsider jurisprudence" was first used by
Professor Mari Matsuda. *See* Mari J. Matsuda, *Public Response to Racist Speech:
Considering the Victim's Story,* 87 M I C H. L. R E V. 2320, 2323 (1989). Here, the
term is preceded with "critical" to emphasize this key feature of the body of work
to which LatCrit theory belongs.

6 *See* Athena D. Mutua, *The Rise, Development, and Future Directions of Critical
Race Theory and Related Scholarship,* 84 D E N V E R U. L. R E V. 329 (2006) ("White
scholars were excluded from participating in the [annual CRT] workshop, a

decision which generated debate as to whether this was a pragmatic attempt to construct safe space and inhibit the reproduction of white racial hierarchy, or simply an unprincipled decision. In either case, the question became moot with the cessation of annual CRT workshops and the almost simultaneous founding of the annual LatCrit conferences with [LatCrit's] commitment to antiessentialist practice and its open-door policy that welcomed whites.").

7 Kevin R. Johnson, *Roll Over Beethoven: "A Critical Examination of Recent Writing About Race,"* 82 TEX. L. REV. 717, 732 (2004).

8 Angela P. Harris, *Building Theory, Building Community,* 8 SOC. & LEGAL STUD. 313 (1999).

9 The "OutCrit" denomination is not an effort to name a new or distinct school of legal scholarship but rather signifies a grouping of existing efforts based on shared commonalities, ranging from feminism and Critical Race Theory to LatCrit, ClassCrits, and Queer studies. "OutCrit" refers (at least initially) to those scholars who identify and align themselves with outgroups in this country, as well as globally, including most notably those who in recent times have launched lines of critical inquiry within legal culture, including critical legal studies. Thus, while "outsider jurisprudence" may be, but is not always nor necessarily, "critical" in perspective, the OutCrit stance is, by definition, critical in nature. OutCrit positionality is a response to the mutually reinforcing systems of subordination and domination that construct both outgroups and ingroups, and OutCrit scholarship provides a jurisprudential context for LatCrit's own contributions. For further discussion of this designation, *see* Francisco Valdes, *Outsider Scholars, Legal Theory and OutCrit Perspectivity: Postsubordination Vision as Jurisprudential Method,* 49 DEPAUL L. REV. 831 (2000).

10 Mutua, *Rise, Development, and Future Directions,* at 331.

11 For example, in recent years CRT conferences have been regularly organized by Yale law student of color organizations, with those events open to the public, and including a number of longtime CRT and LatCrit scholars as speakers.

12 Mutua, *Rise, Development, and Future Directions,* at 331.

13 From the inception of this jurisprudential experiment, LatCrit theorists have endeavored to learn from prior or concurrent jurisprudential efforts and thus have developed practices designed to ensure that our work is grounded in the cumulative insights of critical outsider jurisprudence. As described in chapter 4, this effort to "perform the theory" includes practices such as "rotating the center" of our programmatic lines of inquiry and creating multiyear "streams of programming" to ensure that critical attention is focused on the varied specific aspects of subordinations as well as on the interlocking nature of systems of subordination based on race, ethnicity, gender, class, sexuality, religion, geography, physical ability, and similar axes of identity. *See, e.g.,* Margaret E. Montoya, *LatCrit Theory: Mapping Its Intellectual and Political Foundations and*

Future Self-Critical Directions, 53 U. MIAMI L. REV. 1119 (1999) (situating LatCrit politically, historically, and intellectually); Kevin R. Johnson, *Celebrating LatCrit Theory: What Do We Do When the Music Stops?*, 33 U.C. DAVIS L. REV. 753 (2000) (reviewing the essays of the LatCrit IV symposium and evaluating LatCrit methodologies to identify some of the challenges facing LatCrit scholars); Athena D. Mutua, *Shifting Bottoms and Rotating Centers: Reflections on LatCrit III and the Black/White Paradigm*, 53 U. MIAMI L. REV. 1177 (1988) (discussing and assessing LatCritical techniques and methods of analysis and praxis in the context of the LatCrit III conference); Francisco Valdes, *Theorizing "OutCrit" Theories: Coalitional Method and Comparative Jurisprudential Experience—RaceCrits, QueerCrits, LatCrits*, 53 U. MIAMI L. REV. 1265, 1299–1306 (1999) (discussing these and similar practices); *see also* Kevin R. Johnson & George A. Martinez, *Crossover Dreams: The Roots of LatCrit Theory in Chicana/o Studies, Activism and Scholarship*, 53 U. MIAMI L. REV. 1143, 1150–61 (1999) (reviewing LatCrit methodologies and premises in relationship to other civil rights movements, in particular Chicana/o scholarship and activism); Montoya, *LatCrit at Ten*, at 121–27 (reviewing the techniques, and the precursors and origins, of LatCrit theory and method); Stephanie L. Phillips, *The Convergence of the Critical Race Theory Workshop with LatCrit Theory: A History*, 53 U. MIAMI L. REV. 1247, 1248–54 (1999) (analyzing and comparing the methods and experiences of the Critical Race Theory Workshops that preceded the emergence of LatCrit events to those of the annual LatCrit conferences to adduce the continuities between the two); Dorothy E. Roberts, *BlackCrit Theory and the Problem of Essentialism*, 53 U. MIAMI L. REV. 855 (1998) (describing critical approaches to the study of "blackness" within or through LatCrit theory).

14 Valdes, *Theorizing "OutCrit" Theories*, at 1294, 1305–06.
15 Tayyab Mahmud, Athena Mutua & Francisco Valdes, *LatCrit Praxis @ XX: Toward Equal Justice in Law, Education, and Society*, 90 CHI.-KENT L. REV. 361, 401 (2015).

2. FOUNDATIONS

Epigraph: Steven W. Bender & Francisco Valdes, with Shelley Cavalieri, Jasmine Gonzalez Rose, Saru Matambanadzo, Roberto Corrada, Jorge Roig, Tayyab Mahmud, Zsea Bowmani & Anthony E. Varona, *Afterword—What's Next? Into a Third Decade of LatCrit Theory, Community, and Praxis*, 16 SEATTLE J. SOC. JUST. 823, 862 (2018) (reprinted with the permission of the Seattle Journal for Social Justice) [hereinafter Bender et al., *What's Next?*].

1 *See* Francisco Valdes, *Under Construction: LatCrit Consciousness, Community, and Theory*, 85 CAL. L. REV. 1087 (1997), 10 LA RAZA L.J. 1 (1998) (pin citations below are to CAL. L. REV.); Valdes, *Theorizing "OutCrit" Theories* (describing LatCrit origins, principles, purposes, and practices).

2 *See* Berta Esperanza Hernández-Truyol, *The Gender Bend: Culture, Sex, and Sexuality—A LatCritical Human Rights Map of Latina/o Border Crossings*, 83 IND. L.J. 1283 (2008).

3 *See* Valdes, *Under Construction*, at 1093.

4 *Ibid.*

5 *Ibid.*

6 *Ibid.* at 1094.

7 *Ibid.*

8 *See* Margaret E. Montoya & Francisco Valdes, *"Latinas/os" and the Politics of Knowledge Production: LatCrit Scholarship and Academic Activism as Social Justice Action*, 83 IND. L.J. 1197, 1204 n.19 (2008) (discussing the conceptual errors in a published critique of LatCrit to include the attempt to "break apart" these functions into separate goals, rather than as these goals were intended and have been carried out by the LatCrit community—as operating "synergistically, and to be approached or pursued thusly").

9 For an early assessment of LatCrit "guideposts" as reflected in the proceedings of the LatCrit I conference, *see* Francisco Valdes, *Poised at the Cusp: LatCrit Theory, Outsider Jurisprudence and Latina/o Self-Empowerment*, 2 HARV. LATINO L. REV. 1, 52–59 (1997) (introducing the papers and proceedings of the first LatCrit conference). These guideposts (and the functions described earlier) are interrelated and, in their operation, interactive. Ideally, they yield synergistic effects. They represent, as a set, the general sense of this project as reflected in the collective writings of the symposium based on the LatCrit I conference. In addition to the seven guideposts noted above, an eighth was originally presented as a "final observation" based on the preceding seven, "acknowledging the relationship of LatCrit to Critical Race Theory," and, in particular, the "intellectual and political debt that LatCrit theorizing owes to Critical Race theorists." *Ibid.* at 57–60.

10 *See* George Martinez, *Legal Indeterminacy, Judicial Discretion and the Mexican-American Litigation Experience: 1930–1980*, 27 U.C. DAVIS L. REV. 555 (1994).

11 *See* Berta Hernandez-Truyol, Angela P. Harris & Francisco Valdes, *Afterword—Beyond the First Decade: A Forward-Looking History of LatCrit Theory, Community and Praxis*, 26 CHICANO-LATINO L. REV. 237 (2006).

12 *See generally ibid.* at 265–67.

13 *See* Valdes, *Poised at the Cusp*, at 53; *see also* Steven W. Bender & Francisco Valdes, *Afterword—At and Beyond Fifteen: Mapping LatCrit Theory, Community, and Praxis*, 14 HARV. LATINO L. REV. 397 (2011).

14 On "rebellious lawyering," *see* GERALD P. LOPEZ, REBELLIOUS LAWYERING: ONE CHICANO'S VISION OF PROGRESSIVE LAW PRACTICE (1992); *see generally* Francisco Valdes, *Rebellious Knowledge Production, Academic Activism, & Outsider Democracy: From Principles to Practices in LatCrit Theory, 1995 to 2008*, 8 SEATTLE J. SOC. JUST. 131 (2009) (relating the concept to LatCrit knowledge production and praxis).

15 Valdes, *Poised at the Cusp*, at 53.
16 *Ibid.* at 53–54.
17 *Ibid.* at 54.
18 *Ibid.* at 55–56.
19 *Ibid.*
20 In broad terms, decolonization "entails the ability of the formerly colonized to exercise their right to self-determination and, thus, is a process that must be envisioned and implemented from the ground up." Natsu Taylor Saito, *Tales of Color and Colonialism: Racial Realism and Settler Colonial Theory*, 10 FLA. A&M U.L. REV. 1, 100 (2014).
21 Valdes, *Poised at the Cusp*, at 57.
22 Valdes, *Under Construction*, at 1107–08 (cautioning against essentialist carelessness in LatCrit discourse that constructs a Latina/o/x subject position within legal theory). As Valdes put it:
     The dangers of essentialist assumptions, articulated forcefully in recent years by various outsider scholars, include the failure to particularize analyses of legal or social conditions, thereby blunting the incisiveness of the scholarship; concepts like multiplicity, intersectionality, and multidimensionality are the analytical tools that vitiate assumed essentialisms in postmodern and outsider discourses. Thus, to essentialize Latinas/os into White and Black groupings in light of existing literature and its lessons would not only replicate the paradigm and its hierarchy but also represent a false social reality: "Latinas/os" are an amalgam comprised not only of diverse races but also of diverse ethnicities, genders, religions, cultures, nationalities, classes, abilities and sexualities. LatCrit essentialism, if we indulge it, would perpetuate the fallacies of the dominant status quo. In sum, if LatCrit theory is to be a relevant and positive force in the lives of Latinas/os in this society, our interrogation of Latina/o identities and positions in Anglo-American contexts, as well as our framing of social and legal issues generally, must resist the pull of essentializing customs and frameworks, including the Black/White paradigm.
23 *See* Derrick A. Bell, Jr., Brown v. Board of Education *and the Interest-Convergence Dilemma*, 93 HARV. L. REV. 518 (1980).
24 Francisco Valdes, *Afterword—Theorizing and Building Critical Coalitions: Outsider Society and Academic Praxis in Local/Global Struggles*, 12 SEATTLE J. SOC. JUST. 983, 1012–21 (2014).
25 Charles R. Lawrence III, *Race, Multiculturalism, and the Jurisprudence of Transformation*, 47 STAN. L. REV. 819 (1995).
26 Cheryl I. Harris, *Whiteness as Property*, 106 HARV. L. REV.1709 (1993).
27 Bell, Brown v. Board of Education.
28 Mari J. Matsuda, *Looking to the Bottom: Critical Legal Studies and Reparations*, 22 HARV. C.R.-C.L. L. REV. 323 (1987).

29 E.g., Robert Westley, *Many Billions Gone: Is it Time to Reconsider the Case for Black Reparations?*, 40 B.C. L. REV. 429 (1998).

30 E.g., CATHERINE A. MACKINNON, FEMINISM UNMODIFIED: DISCOURSES ON LIFE AND LAW (1987).

31 E.g., Alan D. Freeman, *Legitimizing Racial Discrimination through Antidiscrimination Law: A Critical Review of Supreme Court Doctrine*, 62 MINN. L. REV. 1049 (1978); Stephanie Wildman, *The Legitimation of Sex Discrimination: A Critical Response to Supreme Court Jurisprudence*, 63 OR. L. REV. 265 (1984).

32 E.g., Laura E. Gómez, *A Tale of Two Genres: On the Real and Ideal Links Between Law and Society and Critical Race Theory*, in THE BLACKWELL COMPANION TO LAW AND SOCIETY 453 (Austin Sarat ed. 2004).

33 Symposium—*Critical Race Theory: A Commemoration*, 43 CONN. L. REV. 1253 (2011).

34 E.g., LAURA E. GÓMEZ, MANIFEST DESTINIES: THE MAKING OF THE MEXICAN AMERICAN RACE (2007); Adrienne D. Davis, *The Private Law of Race and Sex: An Antebellum Perspective*, 51 STAN. L. REV. 238 (1999); IAN F. HANEY LÓPEZ, WHITE BY LAW: THE LEGAL CONSTRUCTION OF RACE (1996).

35 E.g., MARY DUDZIAK, COLD WAR CIVIL RIGHTS: RACE AND THE IMAGE OF AMERICAN DEMOCRACY (2000).

36 E.g., Richard Delgado, *Minority Law Professors' Lives: The Bell-Delgado Survey*, 24 HARV. C.R.-C.L. L. REV. 349 (1989).

37 We describe the U.S. culture wars briefly in chapter 4 (*see* note 18).

38 E.g., Symposium—*Critical Race Theory and International Law*, 45 VILL. L. REV. 827 (2000); Robert S. Chang & Keith Aoki, *Centering the Immigrant in the Inter/National Imagination*, 85 CAL. L. REV. 1395 (1997), 10 LA RAZA L.J. 309 (1998); Berta Esperanza Hernández-Truyol, *Globalized Citizenship: Sovereignty, Security and Soul*, 50 VILL. L. REV. 1009 (2005).

39 See, e.g., Symposium—*Legal Storytelling*, 87 MICH. L. REV. 2073 (1989).

40 See Delgado, *Imperial Scholar*; Montoya & Valdes, *"Latinas/os" and Latina/o Legal Studies*.

41 See *infra* chapter 4 for discussion of the democratic model of LatCrit.

42 Jerome M. Culp, Jr., Angela P. Harris & Francisco Valdes, *Subject Unrest*, 55 STAN. L. REV. 2435, 2445–46 (2003).

43 See Owen M. Fiss, *Groups and the Equal Protection Clause*, 5 J. PHIL. & PUB. AFFAIRS 107 (1976).

44 See Paul Brest, *In Defense of the Antidiscrimination Principle*, 90 HARV. L. REV. 1 (1976) (articulating the principle and reviewing the Supreme Court's elaboration and application of it).

45 See, e.g., *Parents Involved in Community Schools v. Seattle School District No. 1*, 551 U.S. 701 (2007). See also Angela Mae Kupenda, *(Re)complexioning a Simple Tale: Race, Speech, and Colored Leadership*, 48 CAL. WEST. L. REV. 399 (2012).

46 For a discussion of antisubordination as a successor to antidiscrimination in the context of critical outsider jurisprudence, *see* Culp et al., *Subject Unrest*, at 2449.

47 This discussion is adapted from the *Critical Justice* textbook, as overviewed *infra* at chapter 6.

48 Owen Fiss, *Groups and the Equal Protection Clause*, in EQUALITY AND PREFERENTIAL TREATMENT: A PHILOSOPHY AND PUBLIC AFFAIRS READER 84, 106 (Marshall Cohen, Thomas Nagel & Thomas Scanlon eds. 1977).

49 Culp et al., *Subject Unrest*, at 2442–45; *see generally* Osagie K. Obasogie, *Can the Blind Lead the Blind? Rethinking Equal Protection Jurisprudence Through an Empirical Examination of Blind People's Understanding of Race*, 15 U. PA. J. CONST. L. 705 (2013) (confronting the impossibility of colorblindness socially and doctrinally).

50 *See* Angela P. Harris, *Race and Essentialism in Feminist Legal Theory*, 42 STAN. L. REV. 581 (1990).

51 Elizabeth M. Iglesias & Francisco Valdes, *Expanding Directions, Exploding Parameters: Culture and Nation in LatCrit Coalitional Imagination*, 5 MICH. J. RACE & L. 787, 815–16 and 33 U. MICH. J.L. REFORM 203, 231–32 (2000).

52 *See* Kimberlé Crenshaw, *Demarginalizing the Intersection of Race and Sex: A Black Feminist Critique of Antidiscrimination Doctrine, Feminist Theory and Antiracist Politics*, 1989 U. CHI. LEGAL F. 139 (1989); Kimberlé Crenshaw, *Mapping the Margins: Intersectionality, Identity Politics, and Violence Against Women of Color*, 43 STAN. L. REV. 1241 (1991).

3. LATCRIT CONTRIBUTIONS TO OUTCRIT JURISPRUDENCE
Epigraph: Shelley Cavalieri, in Bender et al., *What's Next?*, at 831.

1 *See, e.g.*, Angela P. Harris, *Foreword—The Unbearable Lightness of Identity*, 2 AFR. AM. L. & POL'Y REP. 207 (1995). On the emergence of a LatCrit subject position, *see* Valdes, *Poised at the Cusp*. For other early or contemporary accounts, *see* Berta Esperanza Hernández-Truyol, *Indivisible Identities: Culture Clashes, Confused Constructs and Reality Checks*, 2 HARV. LATINO L. REV. 199, 200–05 (1997); *see also* Montoya, *LatCrit Theory*; Johnson & Martinez, *Crossover Dreams*; Iglesias & Valdes, *Religion, Gender, Sexuality*.

2 *See, e.g.*, Keith Aoki, *Language Is a Virus*, 53 U. MIAMI L. REV. 968 (1999) (noting extent of Asian American participation in LatCrit conferences and community); Barbara J. Cox, *Coalescing Communities, Discourses and Practices: Synergies in the Anti-Subordination Project*, 2 HARV. LATINO L. REV. 473 (1997) (reflecting on relevance of LatCrit project to white lesbians); Jerome McCristal Culp, Jr., *Latinos, Blacks, Others and the New Legal Narrative*, 2 HARV. LATINO L. REV. 479 (1997) (reflecting on relevance of LatCrit project to African Americans); Stephanie M. Wildman, *Reflections on Whiteness & Latina/o Critical Theory*, 2 HARV. LATINO L. REV. 307 (1997) (reflecting on the significance of the LatCrit project from a white critical feminist perspective).

The "sameness" and "difference" discourse has attracted the attention of many scholars. *See, e.g.*, MARTHA MINOW, MAKING ALL THE DIFFERENCE: INCLUSION, EXCLUSION AND AMERICAN LAW (1990); *see also* Regina Austin, *Black Women, Sisterhood, and the Difference/Deviance Divide*, 26 NEW ENG. L. REV. 877 (1992); Martha Albertson Fineman, *Feminist Theory in Law: The Difference It Makes*, 2 COLUM. J. OF GENDER & L. 1 (1992); Joan C. Williams, *Dissolving the Sameness/Difference Debate: A Post-Modern Path Beyond Essentialism in Feminist and Critical Race Theory*, 1991 DUKE L.J. 296 (1991). The collective effort to mint concepts like antiessentialism, multiplicity, intersectionality, co-synthesis, wholism, interconnectivity, multidimensionality and the like thus also reflects a similar grappling with issues of sameness and difference in various genres of contemporary critical legal theory.

3 LatCrit scholarship and events engaged this point from the start. *See, e.g.*, Haney López, *Race, Ethnicity, Erasure*, at 1158–79; George A. Martinez, *The Legal Construction of Race: Mexican-Americans and Whiteness*, 2 HARV. LATINO L. REV. 321 (1997). We have confronted the internal reproduction of white supremacy within and among Latinas/os/x. *See, e.g.*, Kevin R. Johnson, *"Melting Pot" or "Ring of Fire"?: Assimilation and the Mexican-American Experience*, 85 CAL. L. REV. 1259 (1997), 10 LA RAZA L.J. 173 (1998). We have learned that among Latinas/os/x, as among other groups, those of the nonwhites who are more pale are structurally and systematically more likely to receive the social and material benefits associated with whiteness. *See, e.g., ibid.*, 85 CAL. L. REV at 1287–88 (noting the correlation of skin color to socioeconomic success among various Latina/o/x groups in the United States). In doing this and more, we also have ascertained that racial formation among Latinas/os/x is indeed "different" than among African Americans, Asian Americans, and other racialized, nonwhite groups in the United States, though in many ways it is similar as well. *See, e.g.*, Robert S. Chang, *Toward an Asian American Legal Scholarship: Critical Race Theory, Post-Structuralism, and Narrative Space*, 81 CAL. L. REV. 1241, 1255–58 (1993) (discussing nativistic racism and its dynamics); *see also* Robert S. Chang, *The Nativist's Dream of Return*, 9 LA RAZA L.J. 55 (1996).

4 Many scholars have contributed to the construction of current standards and techniques in the continuing elaboration of critical outsider jurisprudence. For key early contributions, *see* Crenshaw, *Mapping the Margins*; Harris, *Race and Essentialism*; Mari J. Matsuda, *When the First Quail Calls: Multiple Consciousness as Jurisprudential Method*, 11 WOMEN'S RTS. L. REP. 7 (1989); *see also* Crenshaw, *Demarginalizing the Intersection of Race and Sex*. Since then various CRT and LatCrit scholars have continued to develop concepts and tools of critical legal theory to build on these foundational concepts, striving progressively to better capture the dynamics of top-down "identity politics" in law and society. *See, e.g.*, e. christi cunningham, *The Rise of Identity Politics I:*

The Myth of the Protected Class in Title VII Disparate Treatment Cases, 30 U.
CONN. L. REV. 441 (1998) (on wholism); Berta Esperanza Hernández-Truyol,
Building Bridges: Bringing International Human Rights Home, 9 LA RAZA L.J.
69 (1996) (on multidimensionality); Peter Kwan, *Jeffrey Dahmer and the
Cosynthesis of Categories*, 48 HASTINGS L.J. 1257 (1997) (on cosynthesis);
Francisco Valdes, *Sex and Race in Queer Legal Culture: Ruminations on
Identities & Inter-Connectivities*, 5 S. CAL. REV. L. & WOMEN'S STUD. 25
(1995) (on interconnectivity); *see generally* Lawrence, *Race, Multiculturalism
and the Jurisprudence of Transformation*, at 834–35 (1995) (urging greater
efforts along these lines to promote multifaceted projects of social
transformation).

5   As noted earlier, the OutCrit designation signifies a grouping of the various
strands or genres of critical outsider jurisprudence, including feminism, Critical
Race Theory, queer legal theory, LatCrit, Class Crits, disability legal studies, and
others. These different bodies of literature overlap, learn from each other, and
share a "critical" and "outsider" perspective rooted in antisubordination values.
As one whole, these "schools" of legal inquiry amount to an OutCrit network
through which similar ideas, techniques, and people travel and develop.

6   *See, e.g.*, Francisco Valdes, *Race, Ethnicity and Hispanismo in a Triangular
Perspective: The "Essential Latina/o" and LatCrit Theory*, 48 UCLA L. Rev. 305
(2000); *see generally* Montoya & Valdes, *Latinas/os and Latina/o Legal Studies*,
at 194–98.

7   *See* Hernandez-Truyol et al., *Beyond the First Decade*, at 188–93.

8   Tayyab Mahmud, in Bender et al., *What's Next?*, at 861–62.

9   Based on Hernandez-Truyol et al., *Beyond the First Decade*, at 187–93.

10   Enid Trucios-Haynes, *Why "Race Matters:" LatCrit Theory and Latina/o Racial
Identity*, 12 LA RAZA L.J. 1, 1, 6 (2001). Consistent with Trucios-Haynes's article,
LatCrit scholarship has also explored racialization of "different" groups and
social identities in other former European colonies. For instance, LatCrit
programs generated texts on Brazil where "unlike in the United States, what it
means to be Black is not a matter of perceived ancestry or hereditary difference;
rather, it is a matter of color, phenotype, hair texture, class status, and educa-
tional attainment." Robert Westley, *Can Affirmative Action and Reparations
Co-Exist?*, 21 NAT'L BLACK L.J. 155 (2008) (noting that in Brazil, "money
whitens"); *see also* Denise Ferreira da Silva, *The End of Brazil: An Analysis of the
Debate on Racial Equity on the Edges of Global Market Capitalism*, 21 NAT'L
BLACK L.J.169 (2008); Seth Racusen, *Fictions of Identity and Brazilian
Affirmative Action*, 21 NAT'L BLACK L.J. 188 (2008); Tanya M. Washington, *All
Things Being Equal: The Promise of Affirmative Efforts to Eradicate Color-Coded
Inequality in the United States and Brazil*, 21 NAT'L BLACK L.J. 7 (2008). The
appendices point to other locales outside of the United States where we have held
similar programs and events.

11 *See* discussion and citations at note 5, chapter 1, and Luis Angel Toro, *"A People Distinct from Other": Race and Identity in Federal Indian Law and the Hispanic Classification in OMB Directive No. 15*, 26 TEXAS TECH. L. REV. 1219 (1995) (critiquing the ramifications of the current labeling system in the United States, which "lumps together all people who can connect themselves to some 'Spanish origin or culture' together as 'Hispanics'").

12 *See infra* notes 14–20, chapter 3 and sources cited therein on these topics.

13 For a critical discussion of "hispanismo" as a form of identity ideology that helps to explain this essentialization, *see* Valdes, *Race, Ethnicity and Hispanismo*.

14 For a sampling of early readings on race, ethnicity, and identity in LatCrit theory, *see* Robert S. Chang, *Racial Cross-Dressing*, 2 HARV. LATINO L. REV. 423 (1997); Chang & Aoki, *Centering the Immigrant*; Ian Haney López, *Race, Ethnicity, Erasure: The Salience of Race to LatCrit Theory*, 85 CAL. L. REV. 1143 (1997), 10 LA RAZA L.J. 57 (1998); Johnson, *"Melting Pot" or "Ring of Fire?"*; Cheryl Little, *Intergroup Coalitions and Immigration Politics: The Haitian Experience in Florida*, 53 U. MIAMI L. REV. 717 (1999); Guadalupe T. Luna, *On the Complexities of Race: The Treaty of Guadalupe Hidalgo and Dred Scott v. Sandford*, 53 U. MIAMI L. REV. 691 (1999); George A. Martinez, *African-Americans, Latinos and the Construction of Race: Toward an Epistemic Coalition*, 19 CHICANO-LATINO L. REV. 213 (1998); Imani Perry, *Of Desi, J.Lo and Color Matters: Critical Race Theory and the Architecture of Race*, 52 CLEV. ST. L. REV. 139 (2005); Rachel F. Moran, *Neither Black Nor White*, 2 HARV. LATINO L. REV. 61 (1997); Juan F. Perea, *The Black/White Binary Paradigm of Race: The "Normal Science" of American Racial Thought*, 85 CAL. L. REV. 1213 (1997), 10 LA RAZA L.J. 127 (1998); Laura E. Gómez, *Constructing Latina/o Identities*, 19 CHICANO-LATINO L. REV. 187 (1998); for a book-length development of this early reading *see also* GÓMEZ, MANIFEST DESTINIES.

In addition, a cluster of essays in the LatCrit V symposium was focused on comparative racialization. For a discussion of those essays, *see* Kevin R. Johnson, *Comparative Racialization: Culture and National Origin in Latina/o Communities*, 78 DENVER U. L. REV. 633 (2001). For other recent readings on comparative racialization in the United States and Latin America, *see* Taunya Lovell Banks, *Colorism: A Darker Shade of Pale*, 47 UCLA L. REV. 1705 (2000); Neil Gotanda, *Comparative Racialization: Racial Profiling and the Case of Wen Ho Lee*, 47 UCLA L. REV. 1689 (2000); Tanya Kateri Hernandez, *Multiracial Matrix: The Role of Ideology in Enforcement of Antidiscrimination Laws, A United States-Latin America Comparison*, 87 CORNELL L. REV. 1093, 1133–44 (2002).

Efforts to engage Native and Indigenous communities date back to the very first conference, but it was not until LatCrit III in Miami that a "stream" of programming began with a concurrent panel on "Race, Nation and Identity: Indigenous Peoples and LatCrit Theory." At LatCrit IV in Lake Tahoe, a combination of a plenary panel and a workshop were presented on Latina/o/x mestizaje and Indigenous populations, as well as a concurrent panel on "Native Cultures, Comparative Values, and Critical Intersections." This stream continued the next year, at LatCrit V in Denver, with a plenary titled "Post/NeoColonialisms in LatCrit Theory: Continuing the Dialogue." In other years, the SNX—South-North Exchange and ICC—International and Comparative Law Colloquium programs, and the publications based on them, continued this stream in international or hemispheric framings. *See* appendices with programs and publications.

While Asian-Latina/o/x relationships have received extended attention as part of the race/ethnicity LatCrit discourse, programmatic events focused on Filipina/o/x populations and issues have been difficult to sustain. Perhaps the most notable LatCrit program events focused on Filipina/o/x issues took place in Lake Tahoe, when LatCrit IV featured several Filipina/o/x-oriented events, including a keynote address by Filipino scholar Oscar V. Campomanes. *See* Victor C. Romero, *"Aren't You Latino?": Building Bridges Upon Common Misperceptions*, 33 U.C. DAVIS L. REV. 837 (2000) (situating Filipinas/os/x in LatCrit theory).

15 An early example of a spontaneous eruption during the LatCrit II conference in San Antonio focused on the role of religion and spirituality within a jurispruden-tial movement devoted to antisubordination politics, such as LatCrit theory. That eruption, taking place in real time spontaneously on site during the conference, is captured in the symposium of those proceedings. For some of the essays flowing from that encounter, *see* Emily Fowler Hartigan, *Disturbing the Peace*, 19 CHICANO-LATINO L. REV. 479 (1998); Nancy K. Ota, *Falling From Grace: A Meditation on LatCrit II*, 19 CHICANO-LATINO L. REV. 437 (1998); Reynaldo Anaya Valencia, *On Being an "Out" Catholic: Contextualizing The Role of Religion at LatCrit II*, 19 CHICANO-LATINO L. REV. 449 (1998). For a discussion of these essays, and of religion in LatCrit theory, *see* Margaret E. Montoya, *Religious Rituals and LatCrit Theorizing*, 19 CHICANO-LATINO L. REV. 417 (1998). Both the live exchange and published texts illustrated another key axis of diversity within Latina/o/x communities and helped us launch a "stream" of programming over the next several years focused on the intersection between religion and critical outsider jurisprudence. Thus, for example, Plenary Panel One at LatCrit III in Miami was titled "Between/Beyond Colors: Outsiders Within Latina/o Communities" and included presentations focused on Latina/o/x religious diversities, while Patricia Fernandez-Kelly delivered a keynote address on "Santeria in Hialeah: Religion as Cultural Resistance" that explored the sociology of non-Western religious beliefs and practices in the working-class and predomi-nantly Cuban city of Hialeah, Florida; *see also* Berta Esperanza Hernández-Truyol, *Latina Multidimensionality and LatCrit Possibilities: Culture, Gender and Sex*, 53 U. MIAMI. L. REV. 811, 818–24 (1999) (exploring similar

particularities in that same conference program and symposium). The following year in Lake Tahoe, the LatCrit IV program opened with a religious ceremony based on pre-Columbian rites of the Aztec people and featured a concurrent panel on "Religion, Gender and Sexuality: Conscience in LatCrit Theory" that produced various essays on religion and LatCrit theory. *See* Symposium, *Rotating Centers, Expanding Frontiers: LatCrit Theory and Marginal Intersections*, 33 U.C. DAVIS L. REV. 751 (2000). Specifically, that symposium includes a "cluster" of essays devoted to this topic. *See* Guadalupe T. *Luna, Gold, Souls and Wandering Clerics: California Missions, Native Californians and LatCrit Theory*, 33 U.C. DAVIS L. REV. 921 (2000); Laura M. Padilla, *Latinas and Religion: Subordination or State of Grace?*, 33 U.C. DAVIS L. REV. 973 (2000); Terry Rey, *"The Virgin's Slip is Full of Fireflies": The Multiform Struggle Over the Virgin Mary's Legitimierende Macht in Latin America and Its U.S. Diasporic Communities*, 33 U.C. DAVIS L. REV. 955 (2000). For a discussion of these essays, and more generally of religion in LatCrit theory, *see* Francisco Valdes, *Introduction— Piercing Webs of Power: Identity, Resistance, and Hope in LatCrit Theory and Praxis*, 33 U.C. DAVIS L. REV. 897 (2000). As these readings indicate, today's religious traditions in the Americas—like Euroheteropatriarchy as a whole—were transplanted from Europe and forcibly imposed on Indigenous communities and religions, as part of colonial conquest and domestication. *See* Francisco Valdes, *Unpacking Hetero-Patriarchy: Tracing the Conflation of Sex, Gender and Sexual Orientation to Its Origins*, 8 YALE J.L. & HUMAN. 161, 174–202 (1996) (describing some basic tenets of Euroheteropatriarchal social ideologies); Francisco Valdes, *Identity Maneuvers in Law and Society: Vignettes of a Euro-American Heteropatriarchy*, 71 UMKC L. REV. 377 (2002) (elaborating on Euroheteropatriarchy); *see also* Francisco Valdes, *Afterword—Beyond Sexual Orientation in Queer Legal Theory: Majoritarianism, Multidimensionality, and Responsibility in Social Justice Scholarship Or Legal Scholars as Cultural Warriors*, 75 DENV. U. L. REV. 1409, 1427–28 (1998) and sources cited therein.

16 For example, LatCrit devoted the Ninth Annual LatCrit Conference to cultural warfare; *see supra* note 1, chapter 1 and sources cited therein on LatCrit and the culture wars; *see generally infra* note 18, chapter 4 and sources cited therein on the culture wars.

17 For example, the LatCrit VI symposium included a cluster of essays on Cultural and PostColonial Critiques in LatCrit Theory. For a discussion of these essays, *see* Keith Aoki, *Cluster Introduction: One Hundred Years of Solitude: The Alternate Futures of LatCrit Theory*, 54 RUTGERS L. REV. 1031 (2002). These lines of LatCritical inquiry overlap because they flow from the same set of historical and structural facts: the Latina/o/x "presence" in the lands now known as the United States is due principally to American expansionism and imperialism; the Mexican, Puerto Rican, and some other Latina/o/x communities now in the United States originally did not cross any borders to arrive or migrate here

(although in some instances they did cross and invade Indigenous-occupied territory)—the border crossed them, thereby initiating the dynamics of today.

18 Reflecting the salience of "language" to the racialization and subordination of "Latina/o/x" identities, LatCrit scholars have analyzed the power dynamics of language from various angles. *See, e.g.*, Steven W. Bender, *Direct Democracy and Distrust: The Relationship between Language Law Rhetoric and the Language Vigilantism Experience*, 2 HARV. LATINO L. REV. 145 (1997); William Bratton, *Law and Economics of English Only*, 53 U. MIAMI. L. REV. 973 (1999); Christopher David Ruiz Cameron, *How the Garcia Cousins Lost Their Accents: Understanding the Language of Title VII Decisions Approving English-Only Rules as the Product of Racial Dualism, Latino Invisibility, and Legal Indeterminacy*, 85 CAL. L. REV. 1347 (1997), 10 LA RAZA L.J. 261 (1998); Drucilla Cornell, *The Imaginary of English Only*, 53 U. MIAMI. L. REV. 977 (1999); Sharon K. Hom, *Lexicon Dreams and Chinese Rock and Roll: Thoughts on Culture, Language, Translation as Strategies of Resistance and Reconstruction*, 53 U. MIAMI L. REV. 1003 (1999); Margaret E. Montoya, *Silence and Silencing: Their Centripetal and Centrifugal Forces in Legal Communication, Pedagogy and Discourse*, 5 MICH. J. RACE & L. 847, 33 U. MICH. J. L. REFORM 263 (2000). For a discussion of some of these works, *see* Aoki, *Language Is a Virus*.

19 For instance, in addition to LatCrit XV in Denver which centered the relationship of class to color, and vice versa, in the context of the Great Bush Recession starting in late 2008, the earlier LatCrit V program (also in Colorado) was focused on "Class in LatCrit: Theory and Praxis in a World of Economic Inequality." *See* Symposium, 78 DENV. U. L. REV. 467 (2001). The LatCrit IV symposium, for example, included a cluster of essays on "Forging Identities: Transformative Resistance in the Areas of Work, Class and the Law." For a discussion of these essays, *see* Maria L. Ontiveros, *Introduction*, 33 U.C. DAVIS. L. REV. 1057 (2000). In addition, the LatCrit VI symposium featured a cluster of essays on Class, Economics, and Social Rights. For a discussion of those essays, *see* Jane E. Larson, *Cluster Introduction: Class, Economics and Social Rights*, 54 RUTGERS L. REV. 853 (2002). The South-North Exchange, held in Bogotá in May 2006, focused on "Free Market Fundamentalisms" to frame class construction in global terms. *See* Symposium, *Free-Market Fundamentalisms and LatCrit Theory*, 5 SEATTLE J. SOC. JUST. 2 (2007).

For individual essays on class and related issues published in the LatCrit symposia, *see, e.g.*, Christopher David Ruiz Cameron, *The Labyrinth of Solidarity: Why the Future of the American Labor Movement Depends on Latino Workers*, 53 U. MIAMI L. REV. 1089 (1999); Roberto L. Corrada, *A Personal Re/View of Latino/a Identity, Gender and Class Issues in the Context of the Labor Dispute Between Sprint and La Connexion Familiar*, 53 U. MIAMI L. REV. 1065 (1999) (centering class issues and identities in a searching exploration of the ethical conundrums confronting Latina/o/x professionals); Tanya K. Hernandez, *An*

Exploration of Class-Based Approaches to Racial Justice: The Cuban Context, 33
U.C. Davis L. Rev. 1135 (2000); Mary Romero, *Immigration and the Servant
Problem and the Legacy of the Domestic Labor Debate: Where Can You Find Good
Help These Days!*, 53 U. Miami L. Rev. 1045 (1999).

20 For a sampling of essays in LatCrit symposia addressing immigration *see, e.g.*,
Raquel E. Aldana, *The Subordination and Anti-Subordination Story of the U.S.
Immigrant Experience in the 21st Century*, 7 Nev. L.J. 713 (2007); Michele
Alexandre, *At the Intersection of Post-911 Immigration Practices and Domestic
Policies: Can Katrina Serve As a Catalyst For Change?*, 26 Chicano-Latino
L. Rev. 155 (2006); Elvia R. Arriola, *International Human Rights, Popular Culture,
and the Faces of Despair in INS Raids*, 28 U. Miami Inter-Am. L. Rev. 245
(1997); Robert S. Chang, *Migrations, Citizens and Latinas/os: Sojourner's Truth
and Other Stories*, 55 Fla. L. Rev. 479 (2003); Ming H. Chen, *Alienated: A
Reworking of the Racialization Thesis after September 11*, 18 Am. U. J. Gender
Soc. Pol'y & L. 411 (2009); Virginia P. Coto, *LUCHA, The Struggle for Life:
Legal Services for Battered Immigrant Women*, 53 U. Miami L. Rev. 749 (1999);
César Cuauhtémoc García Hernández, *Of Inferior Stock: The Two-Pronged
Repression of Radical Immigrant Birth Control Advocates at the Turn-of-the-
Twentieth Century*, 20 St. Thomas L. Rev. 513 (2008); César Cuauhtémoc
García Hernández, *Cluster Introduction—Immigrant Outsider, Alien Invader:
Immigration Policing Today*, 48 Cal. W. L. Rev. 231 (2012); Rene Galindo,
*Embodying the Gap between National Inclusion and Exclusion: The "Testimonios"
of Three Undocumented Students at a 2007 Congressional Hearing*, 14 Harv.
Latino L. Rev. 377 (2011); Ruben J. Garcia, *Across the Borders: Immigrant
Status and Identity in Law and LatCrit Theory*, 55 Fla. L. Rev. 511 (2003); Lilian
Jiménez, *America's Legacy of Xenophobia: The Curious Origins of Arizona Senate
Bill 1070*, 48 Cal. W. L. Rev. 279 (2012); Kevin R. Johnson, *"Aliens" and The U.S.
Immigration Laws: The Social and Legal Construction of Nonpersons*, 28 U. Miami
Inter-Am. L. Rev. 263 (1997); Kevin R. Johnson, *Immigration and Latino
Identity*, 19 Chicano-Latino L. Rev. 197 (1998); Robert Koulish, *Blackwater
and the Privatization of Immigration Control*, 20 St. Thomas L. Rev. 462
(2008); Sylvia R. Lazos Vargas, *Emerging Latina/o Nation and the Anti-
Immigration Backlash*, 7 Nev. L.J. 685 (2007); Sylvia R. Lazos Vargas, *The
Immigrant Rights Marches (Las Marchas): Did the "Gigante" (Giant) Wake Up or
Does It Still Sleep Tonight?*, 7 Nev. L.J. 780 (2007); Francine J. Lipman, *Bearing
Witness to Economic Injustices of Undocumented Immigrant Families: A New Class
of "Undeserving" Poor*, 7 Nev. L.J. 736 (2007); Cheryl Little, *InterGroup
Coalitions and Immigration Politics: The Haitian Experience in Florida*, 53 U.
Miami L. Rev. 717 (1999); María Pabón López, *The Phoenix Rises from El
Cenizo: A Community Creates and Affirms a Latino/a Border Cultural Citizenship
through its Language and Safe Haven Ordinances*, 78 Denv. U. L. Rev. 1017
(2001); María Pabón López, *Reflections on Educating Latino and Latina*

Undocumented Children: Beyond Plyler v. Doe, 35 SETON HALL L. REV. 1373
(2005); Lindsay Perez Huber and Maria C. Malagon, *Silenced Struggles: The
Experiences of Latina and Latino Undocumented College Students in California*, 7
NEV. L.J. 841 (2007); Katarina Ramos, *Criminalizing Race in the Name of Secure
Communities*, 48 CAL. W. L. REV. 317 (2012); Lisa Rodriguez Navarro, *An
Analysis of Treatment of Unaccompanied Immigrant and Refugee Children in INS
Detention and Other Forms of Institutionalized Custody*, 19 CHICANO-LATINO
L. REV. 589 (1998); Ediberto Roman, *Introduction: Immigration and the Allure of
Inclusion*, 35 SETON HALL L. REV. 1349 (2005); Mary Romero, *Are Your Papers
in Order?: Racial Profiling, Vigilantes, and "America's Toughest Sheriff"*, 14 HARV.
LATINO L. REV. 337 (2011); Mary Romero & Marwah Serag, *Violation of Latino
Civil Rights Resulting From INS and Local Police's Use of Race, Culture and Class
Profiling: The Case of the Chandler Roundup in Arizona*, 52 CLEV. ST. L. REV. 75
(2005); Victor C. Romero, *The Child Citizenship Act and the Family Reunification
Act: Valuing the Citizen as Well as the Citizen Parent*, 55 FLA. L. REV. 489 (2003);
Marisa Silenzi Cianciarulo, *Modern-Day Slavery and Cultural Bias: Proposals for
Reforming the U.S. Visa System for Victims of International Human Trafficking*, 7
NEV. L.J. 826 (2007); Francisco Valdes, *Diaspora and Deadlock, Miami and
Havana: Coming to Terms with Dreams and Dogmas*, 55 Fla. L. Rev. 283 (2003);
Charles R. Venator Santiago, *Deporting Dominicans: Some Preliminary Findings*,
14 HARV. LATINO L. REV. 359 (2011).

21 Elizabeth M. Iglesias & Francisco Valdes, *Expanding Directions, Exploding
Parameters: Culture and Nation in LatCrit Coalitional Imagination*, 5 MICH.
J. RACE & L. 787, 791–92 and 33 U. MICH. J.L. REFORM 203, 207–08 (2000).

22 Ileana Porras, *Colloquium Proceedings: Panel Three: A LatCrit Sensibility
Approaches the International: Reflections on Environmental Rights as Third
Generation Solidarity Rights*, 28 U. MIAMI INTER-AM. L. REV. 413, 421, 424
(1996).

23 For a sampling of readings on transnationalism and internationalism in LatCrit
theory, *see* Symposium, *International Law, Human Rights and LatCrit Theory*, 28
U. MIAMI INTER-AM. L. REV. 1 (1996–97) (publishing the proceedings of the
first LatCrit International and Comparative Law Colloquium, which took place in
Miami following the LatCrit I conference in San Diego and the pre-LatCrit
colloquium in Puerto Rico); *see also* Max J. Castro, *Democracy in Anti-
Subordination Perspective: Local/Global Intersections: An Introduction*, 53 U.
MIAMI L. REV. 863 (1999); Ivelaw L. Griffith, *Drugs and Democracy in the
Caribbean*, 53 U. MIAMI L. REV. 869 (1999); Hom, *Lexicon Dreams and Chinese
Rock and Roll*; Irwin P. Stotzky, *Suppressing the Beast*, 53 U. MIAMI L. REV. 883
(1999); Ratna Kapur & Tayyab Mahmud, *Hegemony, Coercion and Their Teeth-
Gritting Harmony: A Commentary on Power, Culture, and Sexuality in Franco's
Spain*, 5 MICH. J. RACE & L. 995 (2000); Tayyab Mahmud, *Colonialism and
Modern Constructions of Race: A Preliminary Inquiry*, 53 U. MIAMI L. REV. 1219

(1999); Mario Martinez, *Property as an Instrument of Power in Nicaragua*, 53 U. MIAMI L. REV. 907 (1999); Julie Mertus, *Mapping Civil Society Transplants: A Preliminary Comparison of Eastern Europe and Latin America*, 53 U. MIAMI L. REV. 921 (1999); Ediberto Roman, *Reconstructing Self-Determination: The Role of Critical Theory in the Positivist International Law Paradigm*, 53 U. MIAMI L. REV. 943 (1999); Ediberto Roman, *A Race Approach To International Law (Rail): Is There A Need For Yet Another Critique Of International Law?*, 33 U.C. DAVIS L. REV. 1519 (2000); Hernandez-Truyol, *Building Bridges*.

24 Charles R.P. Pouncy, *Institutional Economics and Critical Race/LatCrit Theory: The Need for a Critical "Raced" Economics*, 54 RUT. L. REV. 841, 841–43 (2002).

25 For a sampling of some early contributions to the LatCrit record from authors who are not U.S. law professors, *see* Ratna Kapur, *Post-Colonial Economies of Desire: Legal Representations of the Sexual Subaltern*, 78 DENV. U. L. REV. 855 (2001); Lisa Sun-Hee Park, *Perpetuation of Poverty Through "Public Charge,"* 78 DENV. U. L. REV. 1205 (2001); K.L. Broad, *Critical Borderlands & Interdisciplinary, Intersectional Coalitions*, 78 DENV. U. L. REV. 1151 (2001); Coto, *LUCHA, The Struggle for Life*; Lyra Logan, *Florida's Minority Participation in Legal Education Program*, 53 U. MIAMI L. REV. 743 (1999); Gema Perez-Sanchez, *Franco's Spain, Queer Nation?*, 5 MICH. J. RACE & L. 943; 33 U. MICH. J. L. REF. 359 (2000); Guerra, *LatCrit y La Des-Colonizacion Nuestra*; Griffith, *Drugs and Democracy in the Caribbean*. Other examples include Aniella Gonzalez, *Being Individuals: A Comparative Look at Relationships, Gender & the Public/Private Dichotomy*, 9 U. MIAMI INT'L & COMP. L. REV. 115 (2001); Angie L. Padin, *Hispanismo as Leverage: LatCrit Questions Spain's Motives*, 9 U. MIAMI INT'L & COMP. L. REV. 165 (2001); Nicholas A. Gunia, *Half the Story Has Never Been Told: Popular Jamaican Music As Antisubordination Praxis*, 33 U.C. DAVIS L. REV. 1333 (2000); Ellen J. Pader, *Space of Hate: Ethnicity, Architecture and Housing Discrimination*, 54 RUTGERS L. REV. 881 (2002); Manuel J. Caro, *Tying Racism in El Ejido To Spanish and European Politics*, 54 RUTGERS L. REV. 893 (2002); Beverly A. Greene, *Heterosexism and Internalized Racism Among African Americans: The Connections and Considerations for African American Lesbians and Bisexual Women: A Clinical Psychological Perspective*, 54 RUTGERS L. REV. 931 (2002); Ward Churchill, *The Law Stood Squarely on Its Head: U.S. Legal Doctrine, Indigenous Self-Determination and the Question of World Order*, 81 OR. L. REV. 663 (2002); Joe R. Feagin, *White Supremacy and Mexican Americans: Rethinking the Black-White Paradigm*, 54 RUTGERS L. REV. 959 (2002); Boaventura de Sousa Santos, *Nuestra America; Reinventing a Subaltern Paradigm of Recognition and Redistribution*, 54 RUTGERS L. REV. 1049 (2002); Deon Erasmus, *"Will She Speak, or Won't She? That is The Question": Comments on the Communal Land Rights Bill*, 16 FLA. J. INT'L. L. 539 (2004); Dominique Legros, *Indigenous Peoples' Self-Determination and the Broken Tin Kettle Music of Human Rights and Liberal Democracy*, 16 FLA. J. INT'L. L. 579 (2004); Jose Maria

Monzon, *Let There Be Justice: The Double Standard of Application of Legal Norms*, 16 FLA. J. INT'L. L. 639 (2004); Karin van Marle, *"Meeting the World Halfway"— The Limits of Legal Transformation*, 16 FLA. J. INT'L. L. 651 (2004); Charles R. Venator Santiago, *Race, Nation-Building and Legal Transculturation During the Haitian Unification Period (1822–1844): Towards a Haitian Perspective*, 16 FLA. J. INT'L. L. 667 (2004); Fred Evans, *Multi-voiced Society: Philosophical Nuances on Rushdie's Midnight's Children*, 16 FLA. J. INT'L. L. 727 (2004); Joshua Price & Maria Lugones, *Encuentros and Desencuentros: Reflections on a LatCrit Colloquium in Latin America*, 16 FLA. J. INT'L. L. 743 (2004); Romero & Serag, *Violation of Latino Civil Rights*; Marta Nunez Sarmiento, *Changes in Gender Ideology Among Professional Women and Men in Cuba Today*, 52 CLEV. ST. L. REV. 173 (2005); Nicholas Espiritu, *(E)Racing Youth: The Racialized Construction of California's Proposition 21 and the Development of Alternate Contestations*, 52 CLEV. ST. L. REV. 189 (2005); Aaron Monty, *Retranslating Differences*, 52 CLEV. ST. L. REV. 255 (2005); Ronald L. Mize, Jr., *Reparations for Mexican Braceros? Lessons Learned from Japanese and African American Attempts at Redress*, 52 CLEV. ST. L. REV. 273 (2005); Antonia Darder, *Schooling and the Empire of Capital: Unleashing the Contradictions*, 50 VILL. L. REV. 847 (2005); Mary Romero, *Revisiting OutCrits with a Sociological Imagination*, 50 VILL. L. REV. 925 (2005); Mary Romero, *Class Struggle and Resistance Against the Transformation of Land Ownership and Usage in Northern New Mexico: The Case of Las Gorras Blancas*, 26 CHICANO-LATINO L. REV. 87 (2006); Maria Clara Dias, *Moral Dimensions of Nationalism*, 50 VILL. L. REV. 1063 (2005); Gil Gott, *The Devil We Know: Racial Subordination and National Security Law*, 50 VILL. L. REV. 1073 (2005).

26 Athena D. Mutua, *The Rise, Development and Future Directions of Critical Race Theory and Related Scholarship*, 84 DENV. U. L. REV. 329, 392 (2006).

27 See *supra* note 19, chapter 3 and sources cited therein on class and inequality.

28 For a good example, *see* Reginald C. Oh, *Mapping a Materialist LatCrit Discourse on Racism*, 52 CLEV. ST. L. REV. 243 (2005); *see also* Elizabeth M. Iglesias & Francisco Valdes, *LatCrit at Five: Institutionalizing a Postsubordination Future*, 78 DENV. U. L. REV. 1249, 1251–55 (2001).

29 Mahmud et al., *Foreword: LatCrit Praxis*, at 374; *see also* Mutua, *Rise, Development, and Future Directions*, at 331 n.8 (noting the term "ClassCrits" reflected the "interest in focusing on economics through the lens of critical legal scholarship movements, such as critical legal studies, critical feminist theory, critical race theory, LatCrit, and queer theory. That is, we start[ed] with the assumption that economics in law is inextricably political and fundamentally tied to questions of systemic status-based subordination.").

30 Mahmud et al., *Foreword: LatCrit Praxis*, at 374, 401–02.

31 *See* Montoya & Valdes, *"Latinas/os" and Latina/o Legal Studies*; *see also* chapter 5 for a discussion of LatCrit praxis interventions.

32 *E.g.*, Carmen G. Gonzalez, *Deconstructing the Mythology of Free Trade: Critical Reflections on Comparative Advantage*, 17 BERKELEY LA RAZA L.J. 65 (2006); Tayyab Mahmud, *Colonialism and Modern Constructions of Race: A Preliminary Inquiry*, 53 U. MIAMI L. REV. 1219 (1999).

33 *E.g.*, Neil Gotanda, *A Critique of "Our Constitution is Color-Blind,"* 44 STAN. L. REV. 1 (1991); Charles R. Lawrence, *Two Views of the River: A Critique of the Liberal Defense of Affirmative Action*, 101 COLUM. L. REV. 928 (2001).

34 *E.g.*, Sumi Cho, *Post-Racialism*, 94 IOWA L. REV. 1589 (2009); *see generally* Derrick Bell, *After We're Gone: Prudent Speculations on America in a Post-Racial Epoch*, 34 ST. LOUIS U. L.J. 393 (1990).

4. COMMUNITY AND METHOD

Epigraph: *See* Mutua, *Shifting Bottoms*, at 1178.

1 Athena Mutua offered the "shifting bottoms" metaphor to suggest that many groups suffer from oppression and that they suffer differently: "Specifically, Blacks are at the bottom (the most disadvantaged) of a colorized racial category, although there are other racial categories and perhaps, multiple racial systems. The bottom shifts among these categories and systems, often in relation to particular issues." *See* Mutua, *Shifting Bottoms*, at 1177.

2 Sarudzayi M. Matambanadzo, Francisco Valdes & Sheila Velez, *Afterword— Kindling the Programmatic Production of Critical and Outsider Legal Scholarship, 1996–2016*, 37 WHITTIER L. REV. 439, 448 (2016); *see also* Matsuda, *Looking to the Bottom* (arguing the people at the bottom—those who experience discrimination—should be the source of normative law); *see generally* DERRICK BELL, FACES AT THE BOTTOM OF THE WELL (1992) (examining racial hierarchy in the United States "from the bottom").

3 Mutua, *Shifting Bottoms*, at 1204–06, 1208, 1216.

4 *See* Jerome M. Culp, Jr., *Latinos, Blacks, Others, and the New Legal Narrative*, 2 HARV. LATINO L. REV. 479, 481 (1997).

5 *See, e.g.*, Haney López, *Race, Ethnicity, Erasure*; see *also infra* note 14, chapter 3 and sources cited therein on race and ethnicity in LatCrit theory.

6 Montoya & Valdes, *"Latinas/os" and Latina/o Legal Studies*, at 1220 (reflection from LatCrit Oral Histories project).

7 *See* Richard Delgado, *The Imperial Scholar: Reflections on a Review of Civil Rights Literature*, 132 U. PA. L. REV. 561 (1984).

8 The materials in this section are largely derived from Montoya & Valdes, *"Latinas/ os" and Latina/o Legal Studies*.

9 Because of these features, we adopt "democratic" as the name of this knowledge production model from the work of a long-time LatCrit scholar, Sylvia Lazos Vargas, in a text published in the LatCrit IX symposium. *See* Sylvia R. Lazos Vargas, *"Kulturkampf(s)" or "Fit(s) of Spite"?: Taking the Academic Culture Wars Seriously*, 35 SETON HALL L. REV. 1309 (2005).

10 Marc-Tizoc González, Yanira Reyes-Gil, Belkys Torres & Charles R. Venator-
Santiago, *Afterword—Change and Continuity: An Introduction to the LatCrit
Taskforce Recommendations*, 8 Seattle J. Soc. Just. 303, 308 (2009).

11 Saru Matambanadzo, in Bender et al., *What's Next?*, at 847–48.

12 Zsea Bowmani, in Bender et al., *What's Next?*, at 872–73.

13 A near majority of alumnae of the LatCrit Student Scholar Program successfully
entered teaching in law or related fields: Danielle Boaz (UNC Charlotte,
Department of Africana Studies); Alexia Brunet (Colorado); Cruz Caridad Bueno
(SUNY, Department of Black Studies); Kim Chanbonpin (John Marshall); Sonja
Diaz (Founding Director, UCLA Latino Policy & Politics Initiative); Marc-Tizoc
González (New Mexico); Vinay Harpalani (New Mexico); César García
Hernández (Denver); Ummni Khan (Carleton University); Stephen Lee (UC
Irvine); Jorge Contesse Singh (Rutgers); Spearlt (Thurgood Marshall); Tania
Valdez (Denver); and Rose Cuison Villazor (Hofstra).

14 Jasmine Gonzalez Rose, in Bender et al., *What's Next?*, at 843.

15 For more on Campo Sano, the LatCrit community campus, *see* chapter 7.

16 Francisco Valdes, *LatCrit: A Conceptual Overview*, http://biblioteca.uprrp.edu/
LatCritCD/ConceptualOverview.htm [https://perma.cc/EGU5-XYSJ].

17 *See generally* Symposium, *LatCrit Theory: Naming and Launching a New Discourse
of Critical Legal Scholarship*, 2 Harv. Latino L. Rev. 1 (1997) (publishing the
essays from the First Annual LatCrit Conference).

18 Generally, culture wars and "Kulturkampf" are associated with German politics,
both during the Bismarckian struggle to assert secular state authority over
Catholic dogma in the form of public policy, as well as during the efforts of the
Nazi Party to reform German culture in line with their racist ideology. *See
generally* Richard J. Evans, The Coming of the Third Reich 118–53
(2003) (focusing on the culture wars waged in Germany as part of the Nazi rise to
power). The links between the Third Reich and events in the United States are
complex but clear. James Q. Whitman, Hitler's American Model:
The United States and the Making of Nazi Race Law (2017)
(describing Nazi praise for U.S. white supremacy and intentional Nazi efforts to
learn from the U.S. legal system to make their own more effective and efficient
racially). This concept of cultural warfare has been used within the United States
for several decades to describe campaigns aimed at reversing New Deal and Civil
Rights lawmaking legacies. *See, e.g.*, Chris Black, *Buchanan Beckons Conservatives
to Come "Home,"* Bost. Globe, Aug. 18, 1992, at A12; Paul Galloway, *Divided We
Stand: Today's "Cultural War" Goes Deeper than Political Slogans*, Chi. Trib.,
Oct. 28, 1992, at C1. These culture wars also operate to stifle criticality in general
and critical approaches to legal knowledge production in particular. *See* Francisco
Valdes, *Culture, "Kulturkampf," and Beyond: The Antidiscrimination Principle
Under the Jurisprudence of Backlash*, in The Blackwell Companion to
Law and Society 271 (Austin Sarat ed. 2004) (focusing broadly on three

theoretical perspectives—backlash jurisprudence, liberal legalisms, and critical outsider jurisprudence—to compare their approaches to equality law and policy in the context of backlash "Kulturkampf"). *See supra* note 1, chapter 1 and sources cited therein on LatCrit and the culture wars.

19 Richard Delgado, *Crossroads and Blind Alleys: A Critical Examination of Recent Writing About Race*, 82 TEX. L. REV. 121, 146 (2003).

20 Johnson, *Roll Over Beethoven*, at 732.

21 Jorge Roig, in Bender et al., *What's Next?*, at 867–68.

22 The materials in this Section are based on a discussion in Francisco Valdes, *Afterword: Theory Without Borders: LatCritical Approaches to South-North Legal Frameworks and Hemispheric Justice Studies*, 5 J. RACE, GENDER & POVERTY 1 (No. 2, 2013–14).

23 Valdes, *Rebellious Knowledge Production*, at 148.

24 Some of the works in the LatCrit II symposium reflect this moment from different intragroup perspectives. *See* Symposium, *Difference, Solidarity and Law: Building Latina/o Communities through LatCrit Theory*, 19 CHICANO-LATINO L. REV. 1 (1998).

25 For instance, during the LatCrit I conference the women met alone, and on another occasion, during the LatCrit IV conference, a talking circle involving a group of self-selected participants discussed Indigenous and mestizo identities. Both of these "spontaneous" caucuses help to illustrate the organic and democratic nature of the LatCrit experiment.

26 Roberto Corrada, in Bender et al., *What's Next?*, at 852.

27 Saru Matambanadzo, in Bender et al., *What's Next?*, at 848.

28 *See* chapter 5 for discussion of LatCrit praxis.

29 For a thoughtful discussion of this topic in LatCrit and other genres of critical outsider jurisprudence, *see* Angela P. Harris, *Building Theory, Building Community*, 8 SOC. & LEGAL STUD. 313, 321–22 (1999). This topic also has drawn the attention of LatCrit scholars over the years, who have grappled with sources of "difference" and diversity in our community-building efforts. *See, e.g.,* Alicia G. Abreu, *Lessons From LatCrit: Insiders and Outsiders, All at the Same Time*, 53 U. MIAMI L. REV. 787 (1999) (discussing the author's dual sense of "insider" and "outsider" positionality within LatCrit conferences); Elvia Arriola, *Welcoming the Outsider to an Outsider Conference: Law and the Multiplicities of Self*, 2 HARV. LATINO L. REV. 397 (1997) (viewing LatCrit from an outsider/Latina lesbian perspective); Enrique Carrasco, *Who Are We?*, 19 CHICANO-LATINO L. REV. 331 (1998) (considering the multiple roles or identities of LatCrit scholars); Max J. Castro, *Making Pan Latino: Latino Pan-Ethnicity and the Controversial Case of Cubans*, 2 HARV. LATINO L. REV. 179 (1997) (discussing the peculiar position of Cubans and Cuban Americans in Latina/o/x intergroup relations within the United States); Elizabeth M. Iglesias, *Human Rights in International Economic Law: Locating Latinas/os in the Linkage Debates*, 28 U.

MIAMI INTER-AM. L. REV. 361 (1996) (reflecting on intra-Latina/o/x divisions based on differing degrees of cultural assimilation, nationalist ideologies, as well as race, class, and gender hierarchies and the implications of such "difference" for progressive law reform initiatives); Kevin R. Johnson, *Some Thoughts on the Future of Latino Legal Scholarship*, 2 HARV. LATINO L. REV. 101 (1997) (reflecting on Chicana/o/x, Puerto Rican, and Cuban differences); Victoria Ortiz & Jennifer Elrod, *Reflections on LatCrit III: Finding "Family,"* 53 U. MIAMI L. REV. 1257 (1999) (discussing the role of "safe spaces" from community building within the legal academy in the face of "differences" that affect both the academy as well as society at large); Guadalupe T. Luna, *"La Causa Chicana" and Communicative Praxis*, 78 DENV. U. L. REV. 553 (2001) (theorizing relationship between Chicana/o/x studies and LatCrit theory and our community-building praxis); Ediberto Roman, *Common Ground: Perspectives on Latina-Latino Diversities*, 2 HARV. LATINO L. REV. 483, (1997) (elaborating on commonalities upon which Latinas/os/x may build a sense of constructive collectivity).

30 *See, e.g.*, Fischl, *The Question that Killed Critical Legal Studies* (discussing the cause/s of "death" of Critical Legal Studies); DANIEL A. FARBER & SUZANNA SHERRY, BEYOND ALL REASON: THE RADICAL ASSAULT ON TRUTH IN AMERICAN LAW (1997) (illustrating the attacks on critical and outsider jurisprudence); *see also supra* note 1, chapter 1, and note 18, chapter 4, and sources cited therein, on the U.S. culture wars.

31 *See generally* Culp et al., *Subject Unrest*, at 2440–41 n.14.

32 By "critical coalitions" we mean alliances based on a thoughtful and reciprocal interest in the goal(s) or purpose(s) of the coalition. A "critical" coalition—unlike strategic forms of collaboration—is the sort of collaborative project that results from a careful and caring commitment to the substantive reason(s) for it, and that produces on all sides a reformatory agenda and cooperative dynamic that reflect this mutual commitment. *See* Valdes, *Outsider Scholars*, at 835–38 (on critical coalitions). For further elaboration of this concept, *see* Julie A. Su & Eric K. Yamamoto, *Critical Coalitions: Theory and Praxis*, in CROSSROADS, DIRECTIONS AND A NEW CRITICAL RACE THEORY 379 (Francisco Valdes, Jerome McCristal Culp & Angela P. Harris eds 2002); *see generally* Mari J. Matsuda, *Beside My Sister, Facing the Enemy: Legal Theory Out of Coalition*, 43 STAN. L. REV. 1183, 1189 (1991) (urging antisubordination analyses to "ask the other question" as a means of theorizing across single-axis group boundaries). Related to community-building, this concern over intergroup relations and collaborations has been a consistently important theme in outsider jurisprudence, including LatCrit theory. *See, e.g.*, Johnson, *Some Thoughts on the Future* (discussing the challenges facing LatCrit theory); Martinez, *Toward an Epistemic Coalition* (urging Latinas/os/x, Blacks, and other groups of color to coalesce around "race" and our collective, cumulative knowledge of white supremacy); Roman, *Common Ground*, at 483–84 (urging Latinas/os/x to focus on our

similarities rather than our differences as a way of promoting intra-group justice and solidarity); Eric K. Yamamoto, *Conflict and Complicity: Justice Among Communities of Color*, 2 HARV. LATINO L. REV. 495 (1997) (analyzing inter-group grievances and relations among groups of color); *see also supra* note 29, chapter 4 and sources cited therein on identity, and community- and coalition-building, in the face of "difference" and diversity.

33 Roberto Corrada, in Bender et al., *What's Next?*, at 857.

34 As expressed in the form and structure of the annual and now biennial LatCrit conferences, still our flagship project, this emphasis on community-building is manifest in the "twin pillars" of our approach to personal collective praxis. The commitment to continuity reflects this emphasis in the practice of rotating centers—the act of rotation at each conference represented in a substantive and programmatic way the variegated diversities of the communities from which we hailed, as well the Latina/o/x critical community under construction. The commitment to inclusivity equally reflects this emphasis, as reflected in the participation and themes of the LatCrit conferences over the years. Moreover, the "streams of programming" approach to substantive collective agendas promoted among us an ever better understanding of our "differences" and how we might build communities built on substantive commitments to each other without occluding or distorting those differences.

35 *See* chapter 7 for a discussion of Campo Sano and the Living Justice Institute.

36 Based on Montoya & Valdes, *"Latinas/os" and Latina/o Legal Studies*, at 221.

37 An early example is the SALT C.A.R.E. (Communities Affirming Real Equality) March during the AALS meeting in San Francisco in early 1998. Organized by SALT board members Margaret Montoya and Sumi Cho, who also served on the LatCrit Board, the march by academics, politicians, and civil rights group and community organization members aimed to target the backlash of anti–affirmative action measures in the states, courts, colleges, and society at large by expressing a commitment to diversity and toward a reconstruction of "merit."

38 *See generally* Jean Stefancic, *The Law Review Symposium Issue: Community of Meaning or Re-Inscription of Hierarchy?*, 63 U. COLO. L. REV. 651 (1992).

39 *See* the Appendices C-E below for the programs and publications based on the proceedings of these three projects.

5. LATCRIT PRAXIS

Epigraph: *See* Valdes, *Under Construction*, at 1093.

1 *See* Francisco Valdes, *Insisting on Critical Theory in Legal Education: Making Do While Making Waves*, 12 LA RAZA L.J. 137, 140 (2001). LatCrit's antisubordination commitment and its kinship with CRT led its organizers and community members to consciously pursue both a theory and the practice of coalition-building as well as a theory and application of praxis. *See* Mutua, *Rise, Development and Future Directions*, at 374–76 (2006) (noting the concept is often

termed "antisubordination praxis," to encompass the many justice projects that inform the antisubordination commitment, but that "the idea of coalition and alliances" are a key part of the equation: "critical theorizing should and needs to be informed by practice, by active engagement with developments on the ground while practice should and needs to be informed by theorizing and theories about what is happening, all for the benefit of oppressed communities"). As Mutua and others conclude: "This is best accomplished by these groups working together, theorist and activist, to mutually inform one another's work; and more importantly, to do so on behalf of and in conjunction with communities of color." *Ibid.* at 376. *See also* Eric K. Yamamoto, *Critical Race Praxis: Race Theory and Political Lawyering Practice in Post-Civil Rights America*, 95 MICH. L. REV. 821, 829 (1997).

2 *See Arce v. Douglas*, 793 F.3d 968 (9th Cir. 2015); *see generally* Guadalupe Theresa Luna, *LatCrit Praxis*: Arce v. Huppenthal, 10 CHARLESTON L. REV. 277 (2016).

3 *See Fort Lauderdale Food Not Bombs v. City of Fort Lauderdale*, 901 F.3d 1235 (11th Cir. 2017).

4 LatCrit symposia articles on the subject of policing thus far have tended to focus on police violence impacting Latina/o/x communities. *E.g.*, Romero & Serag, *Violation Of Latino Civil Rights*; Mary Romero, *State Violence, and the Social and Legal Construction of Latino Criminality: From El Bandido to Gang Member*, 78 DENV. U.L. REV. 1081 (2001). *See also* Kevin R. Johnson, *The Case of African American and Latina/o Cooperation in Challenging Racial Profiling in Law Enforcement*, 55 FLA. L. REV. 341 (2003). LatCrit community member publications outside LatCrit symposia have added depth to critiques of policing. *E.g.*, Frank Rudy Cooper, *Cop Fragility and Blue Lives Matter*, 2020 U. ILL. L. REV. 621 (2020); Angela J. Davis, POLICING THE BLACK MAN: ARREST, PROSECUTION AND IMPRISONMENT (2017); Justin Hansford, *Community Policing Reconsidered: From Ferguson to Baltimore*, in POLICING THE PLANET: WHY THE POLICING CRISIS LED TO BLACK LIVES MATTER (Jordan T. Camp and Christina Heatherton eds. 2016); Cynthia Lee, *Making Black and Brown Lives Matter: Incorporating Race into the Criminal Procedure Curriculum*, 60 ST. LOUIS U. L.J. 481 (2016).

5 *See* Tucker Culbertson, *A Report on—and an Invitation to Join—the LatCrit NGO*, 4 FIU L. REV. 73, 73 (2008) (reporting on the NGO's activities and plans).

6 *Ibid.* at 84.

7 Valdes, *Theorizing and Building Critical Coalitions*, at 1020.

8 *See* Valdes, *Insisting on Critical Theory in Legal Education*.

9 *See* Francisco Valdes, *Foreword—Interruptions and Intersections: Journeys to the Center of the Americas*, 4 TENN. J.L. & POL'Y 167 (2008).

10 Consistent with the LatCrit emphasis on streams of programming discussed in chapter 4, we have proactively tried to make the Study Space immersions more than a one-time event. An additional dimension here of critical concern is that

immersion with the bottom in a particular region may require the building and
cultivation of trust that a one-time visit from lawyers and other professionals may
violate. Learning from past errors such as a bus tour of depressed areas in San
Antonio during the LatCrit II conference, the last Study Space in Guatemala set a
standard for ongoing intervention. The Study Space was arranged by LatCrit
community member Raquel Aldana, who had longstanding relationships with the
groups we visited. For the most part, we came to the communities in their own
far-flung meeting spaces (school courtyards, community center verandas, a large
covered area in an alley converted into a community meeting space) rather than
bringing them to a central and formal academic setting. We supported their
community chest by purchasing their art and donating to their causes. After the
Study Space, we held an academic conference at a U.S. law school that brought
together the Study Space participants, with some of the Guatemalan organizations
we visited in attendance. We secured a book publication to disseminate the ideas
and knowledge from the bottom derived from the immersion and the follow-up
conference. And, finally, we held a South-North Exchange at the same site to
continue efforts to learn from, and in some cases to lend aid to, the local
struggles, when and where those community members felt it best. We also
published a symposium following the South-North Exchange and are alert to
ways in which the immersion participants individually, and more so collectively,
can continue contact and involvement with the local issues.

11 Valdes, *Afterword—Theorizing and Building Critical Coalitions*, at 1028.

12 *Ibid.*

13 Berta Esperanza Hernández-Truyol, *International Law, Human Rights and LatCrit Theory: Civil and Political Rights—An Introduction*, 28 U. MIAMI INTER-AM. L. REV. 223, 238, 241 (1997).

14 Hernandez-Truyol et al., *Afterword*, at 239–40.

6. CRITICAL PEDAGOGY

Epigraph: Margaret E. Montoya, *Academic Mestizaje: Re/Producing Clinical Teaching and Re/Framing Wills as Latina Praxis*, 2 HARV. LATINO L. REV. 349, 353 (1997).

1 *See, e.g.*, Marc-Tizoc González, *Education and Pedagogy: Counter-Disciplinarity in the Critical Education Tradition in LatCrit Theory*, 8 SEATTLE J. SOC. JUST. 107 (2009) (introducing the "Education and Pedagogy" symposium cluster of articles based on the LatCrit XIII annual conference, Seattle, WA, October 2008); Marc-Tizoc González, *Tracing the Critical Education Tradition in LatCrit Theory, Praxis & Community*, 4 FIU L. REV. 85 (2008) (introducing the "Critical Education" symposium cluster of articles based on the LatCrit XII annual conference, Miami, FL, October 2007).

2 Charles R. Venator Santiago, *Foreword—Countering Kulturkampf Politics Through Critique and Justice Pedagogy*, 50 VILL. L. REV. 749, 763 (2005).

3 Francisco Valdes, *Barely at the Margins: Race and Ethnicity in Legal Education—A Curricular Study With LatCritical Commentary*, 13 BERKELEY LA RAZA L.J. 119 (2002).

4 For an example of such a LatCrit course taught at the University of Washington School of Law by such faculty as Dean Mario L. Barnes, Brenda Williams, and Edwin Lindo, see www.law.washington.edu/coursecatalog/course. aspx?ID=E571.

5 Aníbal Rosario-Lebrón, *If These Blackboards Could Talk: The Crit Classroom, A Battlefield*, 9 CHARLESTON L. REV. 305, 313 (2015) (summarizing the insights of Paulo Freire and the Frankfurt school).

6 Daniel G. Solórzano & Tara J. Yosso, *Maintaining Social Justice Hopes Within Academic Realities: A Freirean Approach to Critical Race/LatCrit Pedagogy*, 78 DENV. U. L. REV. 595, 596 (2001).

7 Francisco Valdes, *Outsider Jurisprudence, Critical Pedagogy and Social Justice Activism: Marking the Stirrings of Critical Legal Education*, 10 ASIAN L.J. 65, 94–96 (2003); *see also* Valdes, *Insisting on Critical Theory in Legal Education.*

8 Sheila I. Vélez Martínez, *Towards an Outcrit Pedagogy of Anti-subordination in the Classroom*, 90 CHI.-KENT L. REV. 585 (2015).

9 Mario L. Barnes, *LatCrit Theory, Narrative Tradition and Listening Intently for a "Still Small Voice,"* 1 U. MIAMI RACE & SOC. JUST. L. REV. 1, 4 n.10 (2011); *see also* Margaret E. Montoya, *Celebrating Racialized Legal Narratives*, in CROSSROADS, DIRECTIONS, AND A NEW CRITICAL RACE THEORY 243 (Valdes et al. eds. 2002); Mario L. Barnes, *Black Women's Stories and the Criminal Law: Restating the Power of Narrative*, 39 U.C. DAVIS L. REV. 941, 951–57 (2006); Jerome M. Culp, Jr., *Autobiography and Legal Scholarship and Teaching: Finding Me in the Legal Academy*, 77 VA. L. REV. 539 (1991).

10 Angela Harris & Leslie Espinoza, *Afterword—Embracing the Tar-Baby: LatCrit Theory and the Sticky Mess of Race*, 85 CAL. L. REV. 1585, 1585 (1997), 10 LA RAZA L.J. 499, 499 (1998).

11 *See, e.g.*, Lindsay Perez Huber, *Beautifully Powerful: A LatCrit Reflection on Coming to an Epistemological Consciousness and the Power of Testimonio*, 18 AM. U. J. GENDER SOC. POL'Y & L. 839 (2010); *see generally* Venator Santiago, *Countering Kulturkampf*, at 758; Lazos Vargas, *"Kulturkampf(s)" or "Fit(s) of Spite"?*

12 *E.g.*, Richard Delgado, *Rodrigo's Eighth Chronicle: Black Crime, White Fears—On the Social Construction of Threat*, 80 VA. L. REV. 503 (1994).

13 Solórzano & Yosso, *Maintaining Social Justice.*

14 *Ibid.* at 600.

15 Montoya, *Silence and Silencing*, 33 U. MICH. J.L. REF. at 327, 5 MICH. J. RACE & L. at 911.

16 Vélez Martínez, *Towards an OutCrit Pedagogy.*

17 *Ibid.*

18 Rosario-Lebrón, *If These Blackboards*, at 312–13, 322; *see also* SpearIt, *Priorities of Pedagogy: Classroom Justice in the Law School Setting*, 48 CAL. WEST. L. REV. 467 (2012).

19 Vélez Martínez, *Towards an OutCrit Pedagogy*, at 587–88.

20 Roberto L. Corrada, *Toward an Ethic of Teaching: Class, Race and the Promise of Community Engagement*, 50 VILL. L. REV. 837, 841 (2005) (citing Margaret E. Montoya, *Voicing Differences*, 4 CLINICAL L. REV. 147, 153 (1997)).

21 *Ibid.* at 845.

22 Valdes, *Outsider Jurisprudence*, at 86.

23 Originally, the team organized itself into subgroups to develop different parts and chapters of the book. In the years since, those early efforts and results morphed time and again as we tried to figure out how best to do whatever we were trying to do. The original team that launched this project consisted of: Steven Bender, Sumi Cho, Christine Zuni-Cruz, Ibrahim Gassama, Carmen González, Marc-Tizoc González, Gil Gott, Tayyab Mahmud, Margaret Montoya, Athena Mutua, Ileana Porras, Charles Pouncy, and Francisco Valdes. Sheila Vélez Martínez joined the project a few years later. During the past several years through completion, the team has consisted of Steven Bender, Jennifer Hill, and Francisco Valdes.

24 We describe this resource as a textbook rather than a "casebook" because the materials do not rely primarily on judicial opinions deciding cases. Most of the materials consist of edited excerpts from law review articles or other similar sources with editor-composed text bookending them. Case opinions appear from time to time to illustrate specific aspects of systemic injustice and systemic advocacy, rather than for students to puzzle over the "reasoning" of the judges or to memorize the judicial outcomes in order to regurgitate them later.

25 The book consists of seven parts and sixteen chapters that present law as one of many social systems that reproduce collective inequality by institutional design and, frequently, through automatic routines. The textbook is designed to help advocates and activists understand persistent social problems, and solutions to them, in material, systemic, and historical terms that focus on identities, groups, interests, and power. To do so, it presents critical theory as actionable knowledge in diverse social, economic, and legal contexts.

26 Bender et al., *What's Next?*, at 864–65.

27 Although the editors will help teachers to design syllabi for any kind of new or existing course, the commonly offered courses or seminars we have considered in crafting this textbook include those with the following themes or emphases:
Law, Justice, and Power
Law, Systems, and Systemic Advocacy
Law, Lawyering, and Social Change
Law, Identity, and Society
Legal Education and Systemic Injustice
Law, Knowledge, and Social Justice or LRW for Social Justice (research skills)

Law, Policy, and Racialized Materialism
Law, History, and Social Inequality
Law, Society, and Transnational Politics (NAIL/TWAIL)
Law and Critical Theory
Law, Organizing, and Social Change
Law, Ethics, and Systemic Advocacy

As often is the case, no single course is likely to cover the whole book, so the book is designed to help teachers of different courses focus on seven different parts and their respective chapters. Teachers (and other users) are invited to contact the editors, or the LatCrit Board, for help in adapting the materials to your circumstances and goals, as well as to be watchful for syllabus development workshops to be held in conjunction with the LatCrit Community Suite, among other locations.

7. DESIGNING AND SUSTAINING SELF-GOVERNANCE

Epigraph: *See* Articles of Incorporation of Latina and Latino Critical Legal Theory, Inc. (LatCrit, Inc.), a Florida nonprofit corporation, art. 3.2 (filed Mar. 17, 1999), search.sunbiz.org/Inquiry/CorporationSearch/ConvertTiffToPDF? storagePath=COR%5C1999%5C0324%5C90809669.TIF&documentNumber =N99000001806.

1 These early visions were in time distilled into the values and principles, and functions, guideposts, postulates, and hallmarks, that we describe in this Primer. *See* chapter 2.

2 This Conference Planning Manual was spearheaded by law faculty at the University of Denver, including Roberto Corrada and Nancy Ehrenreich.

3 Our formal corporate name as a Florida nonprofit is "Latina and Latino Critical Legal Theory, Inc."

4 The Task Force members were Marc-Tizoc González, Yanira Reyes, Belkys Torres, and Charles R. Venator-Santiago. They published their findings and recommendations over two years in the annual conference-based symposia. *See infra* note 12, chapter 7 and sources cited therein on this process and its conclusions.

5 The move to incorporate was also designed to facilitate the need for formal, institutionalized continuity to help ensure programmatic progression. The corporate form allowed us to pursue the creation of enduring structures that would facilitate substantive, intellectual, and collective continuity while also enabling us to establish a community treasury, which, however modest, would retain any surpluses produced by our various projects or programs as seed money for collective projects. Thus, formal incorporation helped us to secure the conditions both for the ongoing evolution of this critical enterprise as well as a fallback resource to help us sustain the various initiatives that we undertook even when mainstream institutions declined or failed to support us in the ways that they otherwise might or should.

6   To donate, refer to the LatCrit website at https://latcrit.org/donate.

7   Elizabeth M. Iglesias, *Identity, Democracy, Communicative Power, Inter/National Labor Rights and the Evolution of LatCrit Theory and Community*, 53 U. MIAMI L. REV. 575, 647 (1999).

8   Anthony E. Varona, in Bender et al., *What's Next?*, at 890–91.

9   These include the proceedings from the Fourth LatCrit Colloquium on International and Comparative Law (ICC IV), Buenos Aires, Argentina, published in 38 REV. JURÍDICA U. INTER. P.R. 1 (2003) [Revista Jurídica Universidad Interamericana de Puerto Rico, Facultad de Derecho]; *see, e.g.*, Jose Luis Calva, *La Production de Alimentos en Mexico en el Marco de las Politicas Neoliberales y del TLCAN*, 43 U. MIAMI INTER-AM. L. REV. 45 (2011); Miguel Rabago Dorbecker, Graciela Rodriguez, Luis Miguel Cano & Luis Fernando Garcia, *Litigio Estrategico Contra la Siembra de Maiz Geneticamente Modificado en Mexico*, 43 U. MIAMI INTER-AM. L. REV. 269 (2011); Mario Martinez, *La Propiedad Como Instrumento de Poder en Nicaragua*, 53 U. MIAMI L. REV. 913 (1999); Hugo Rojas, *Cambios Socials y Cambios Jurídicos en Chile: Construyendo Nuevos Puentes entre Sociología y Derecho en la Promoción del Realismo Jurídico Latinoamericano*, 13 BERKELEY LA RAZA L.J. 453 (2002); Jonas-Sébastien Beaudry, *La Desigualdad de Género en el Régimen Matrimonial Chileno*, 41 U. MIAMI INTER-AM. L. REV. 187 (2009); Angel Rodriguez-Vergara Diaz, *Evolucion Reciente de la Discriminacion Positiva en el Ambito Laboral y Electoral*, 9 U. MIAMI INT'L & COMP. L. REV. 125 (2000).

10 A long-term goal has been to translate significant portions of the LatCrit symposia and website into Spanish (and, later, Portuguese).

11 Berta E. Hernández-Truyol, *Building Bridges III—Personal Narratives, Incoherent Paradigms, and Plural Citizens*, 19 CHICANO-LATINO L. REV. 303, 314–15 (1998).

12 Marc-Tizoc González, Yanira Reyes, Belkys Torres & Charles R. Venator-Santiago, *The LatCrit Task Force Recommendations: Findings and Recommendations of a Self-Study of the LatCrit Board, 2009*, 18 AM. U. J. OF GENDER SOCIAL POL'Y AND L. 853, 865 (2010) (this 2010 report provided the final Task Force findings and recommendations); *see also* González et al., *Change and Continuity* (this 2009 report was published while the self-study continued).

13 *See, e.g.*, Margaret E. Montoya, *Foreword—Class in LatCrit: Theory and Praxis in a World of Economic Inequality*, 78 DENV. U. L. REV. 467, 470 (2001); Pedro A. Malavet, *Outsider Citizenships and Multidimensional Borders: The Power and Danger of Not Belonging*, 52 CLEV. ST. L. REV. 321, 335 (2005).

14 *See* http://latcrit.org/content/campo-sano.

15 For more information on the LatCrit self-study and strategic planning process of 2008–11, *see supra* chapter 7 and sources cited therein; *see also* Francisco Valdes, *Coming Up: New Foundations in LatCrit Theory, Community and Praxis*, 48 CAL. WEST. L. REV. 505 (2012); appendix A (providing a timeline).

8. LOOKING AHEAD

Epigraph: Anthony E. Varona, in Bender et al., *What's Next?*, at 886.

1 This expansion is managed, in part, through programmatic initiatives that respond to specific aspirations or needs of individuals within the LatCrit community. The process entails discussion and deliberation, but usually, if a group forms itself into a project team to undertake a concrete goal, the LatCrit Board and community at large will be supportive in every possible way.

2 By 2018, the LatCrit Board consisted of Steven Bender, Atiba Ellis, Marc-Tizoc González, Beth Lyon, Saru Matambanadzu, Tayyab Mahmud, Yanira Reyes, Jorge Roig, Francisco Valdes, and Sheila Vélez Martínez. More generally, the project teams planning the FDW, the Biennial LatCrit Conferences, the SNX, and the SSP were composed of and led by more recent generations of scholars, including many of those named above.

3 Anthony E. Varona, in Bender et al., *What's Next?*, at 886–87.

4 *See* Elvia R. Arriola, *Foreword—MARCH!*, 19 CHICANO-LATINO L. REV. 1 (1998).

5 The materials in this Section are based on a discussion in Francisco Valdes, *Afterword: Theory Without Borders: LatCritical Approaches to South-North Legal Frameworks and Hemispheric Justice Studies*, 5 J. RACE, GENDER & POVERTY 1 (No. 2, 2013–14).

6 Sarudzayi M. Matambanadzo, Francisco Valdes & Sheila Velez, *Afterword— Kindling the Programmatic Production of Critical and Outsider Legal Scholarship, 1996–2016*, 37 WHITTIER L. REV. 439, 464–65 (2016).

AFTERWORD

The authors express their gratitude to Margaret Montoya for her helpful insights on this afterword and to Saru Matambanadzo for providing her incisive analysis of the changes in legal education's financial model over LatCrit's two and a half decades. They also thank Frank Valdes and Steven Bender for the Primer's significant contribution to critical legal theory that captures the spirit and substance of the movement known as "LatCrit."

1 MOVEMENT FOR BLACK LIVES, https://m4bl.org/about-us.

2 *See, e.g.*, ELLEN BERREY, THE ENIGMA OF DIVERSITY: THE LANGUAGE OF RACE AND THE LIMITS OF RACIAL JUSTICE 55–78 (2015).

3 For a snapshot of the top fifteen law schools from the late 1980s to 2009, *see* Paul Lomio, Erika V. Wayne & George D. Wilson, *Ranking of Top Law Schools 1987–2009 by US News & World Report*, Robert Crown Law Library Legal Research Paper Series, No. 20 (Apr. 2008), www-cdn.law.stanford.edu/wp-content/uploads/2015/03/lomio_etal-rp20.pdf.

4 In fact, the number of Latinx law faculty was so low that Richard Chused, who published the first Society of American Law Teachers (SALT) survey of faculty demographics, stated he did not break out Latinx faculty into subgroups because

"[t]he number of Hispanic teachers is so low that tabulations other than the gross number of teachers are useless." Richard H. Chused, *The Hiring and Retention of Minorities and Women on American Law School Faculties*, 137 U. PA. L. REV. 537, 538 n.5 (1988). Chused's 1986–87 SALT survey found that only 0.4 percent (12/3303) of tenured classroom law teachers and 1.4 percent (11/800) of tenure-track faculty were "Hispanic." *Id.* at 556.

5 *See id.*, at 558 (Table 4: Number of Minority Faculty Institutional Totals). Nearly another quarter of law schools (excluding HBCUs and Puerto Rican law schools) had only two faculty of color. Taken together, over three-quarters of law schools in 1986–1987 had zero to two faculty of color.

6 For the relationship between law student activism and faculty diversity, *see generally* Sumi Cho & Robert Westley, *Critical Race Coalitions: Key Movements that Performed the Theory*, 33 U.C. DAVIS L. REV. 1377 (2000).

7 For compelling testimony about the perils of such isolation from the first African American female appointed to the tenure track of a predominantly white law school, *see* Joyce A. Hughes, *Neither a Whisper Nor a Shout*, in REBELS IN LAW: VOICES IN HISTORY OF BLACK WOMEN LAWYERS 90–101 (J. Clay Smith, ed. 1998).

8 Daniel Saunders, *Neoliberal Ideology and Public Higher Education in the United States*, 8 J. CRITICAL EDUC. POL'Y STUD., 41, 53 (2010) (internal citations omitted).

9 E. Thomas Sullivan, *The Transformation of the Legal Profession and Legal Education*, 46 IND. L. REV. 145, 146 (2013); Erin J. Cox, *An Economic Crisis Is a Terrible Thing to Waste: Reforming the Business of Law for a Sustainable and Competitive Future*, 57 UCLA L. REV. 511, 520–22 (2009); Larry E. Ribstein, *The Death of Big Law*, 2010 WIS. L. REV. 749, 773 (2010).

10 Sullivan, *Transformation of the Legal Profession*, at 148.

11 Imagine universities or private companies owning the rights to the lectures and PowerPoints of a small number of "superstar" faculty at high-prestige schools and leasing them to cash-strapped law schools, enabling those schools in turn to reduce the size of their tenure-track, full-time faculties. For an example of a new financial arrangement that threatens tenure-track employment, *see, e.g.*, Kevin Carey, *Proposed Merger Blurs the Line Between For-Profit Colleges and Public Universities*, N.Y. TIMES, Aug. 11, 2020, https://nyti.ms/31HO6Rc.

12 Scott Jaschik, *Study: Law Student Aid Likely to Go to White Students*, INSIDE HIGHER EDUC. (Feb. 9, 2017), www.insidehighered.com/quicktakes/2017/02/09/study-law-school-aid-likely-go-white-students (reporting that 80 percent of law student scholarships are not based on financial need but awarded instead to students with high LSAT scores who are disproportionately white).

13 Christopher J. Ryan, Jr., *Paying for Law School: Law Student Loan Indebtedness and Career Choices*, 2021 U. OF ILL. L. REV (forthcoming 2021), ROGER WILLIAMS UNIV. LEGAL STUDIES PAPER NO. 198, 10, Jan. 29, 2020, https://

ssrn.com/abstract=3527863 (finding that law students from underrepresented racial minority groups "account for the largest expected law school debt loads" and that of the students surveyed expected to owe more than $200,000 in law school loans following their graduation, "53 percent identified with a racial group other than white").

14 As Meera Deo, who conducts empirical studies of legal academe, has explained:

For many years AALS maintained basic statistical data on law faculty members by race and gender on its website, including at the following link: http://aalsfar.com/statistics/2009dlt/race.html.

By December 2014, the relevant pages had been removed from the AALS website. In spite of numerous requests by the author of this Article and others for explanation, retrieval, and reinstatement of this data, AALS has not responded in any way and the data remains missing from the AALS website. It is therefore unavailable to those who conduct research on American law faculty. The author welcomes correspondence from anyone with additional information regarding the data or from those who have sought the data to no avail.

Meera Deo, *The Ugly Truth About Legal Academia*, 80 BROOK. L. REV. 943, 947 n.12 (2015).

15 Indeed, junior faculty may not be wrong in this perception: critical race scholars have long argued that contemporary discrimination in white-dominated corporate environments (including law schools) operates on a more subtle level than outright exclusion. Instead, modern employers are simply choosing *among* employees of color, not based primarily on merit (traditional or otherwise) but on such employees' perceived alignment with dominant racial norms and hierarchies. *See generally*, Devon W. Carbado & Mitu Gulati, *Working Identity*, 85 CORNELL L. REV. 1259 (2000); Devon W. Carbado & Mitu Gulati, *The Fifth Black Woman*, 11 J. CONTEMP. LEGAL ISSUES 701 (2001); Devon W. Carbado & Mitu Gulati, *Race to the Top of the Corporate Ladder: What Minorities Do When They Get There*, 61 WASH. & LEE L. REV. 1645 (2004); DEVON W. CARBADO & MITU GULATI, ACTING WHITE? RETHINKING RACE IN POST-RACIAL AMERICA (2013).

16 *See, e.g.*, Jonah Engel Bromwich, *Lawyers Mobilize at Nation's Airports After Trump's Order*, N.Y. TIMES (Jan. 29, 2017), www.nytimes.com/2017/01/29/us /lawyers-trump-muslim-ban-immigration.html; Caitlin Dickerson, *"There Is a Stench": Soiled Clothes and No Baths for Migrant Children at a Texas Center*, N.Y. TIMES (June 21, 2019), /www.nytimes.com/2019/06/21/us/migrant-children-border-soap.html; César Cuauhtémoc García Hernández & Carlos Moctezuma García, *Close Immigration Prisons Now*, N.Y. TIMES, opinion editorial, www .nytimes.com/2020/03/19/opinion/coronavirus-immigration-prisons.html (Mar. 19, 2020); Roshan Nebhrajani, *Meet One of the Lawyers Who Helped Press Pause on the Immigration Ban*, THE NEW TROPIC (Jan. 30, 2017), https://thenewtropic

.com/muneer-ahmad-muslim-immigration-ban/ (profiling the work of legal scholar-activist Muneer I. Ahmad and his students in challenging President Trump's "Muslim ban"); Lisa Weissman-Ward, Q & A with Sharon Driscoll, *Undocumented Immigrants, Sanctuary Jurisdictions and Law*, STANFORD LAW SCHOOL BLOG: LEGAL AGGREGATE (Mar. 9, 2018), https://law.stanford.edu/2018/03/09/undocumented-immigrants-sanctuary-jurisdictions-law.

17 *See, e.g.*, Amna A. Akbar, *The Left is Remaking the World*, N.Y. TIMES, opinion editorial (July 11, 2020), www.nytimes.com/2020/07/11/opinion/sunday/defund-police-cancel-rent.html; Justin Hansford & Meena Jagannath, *Ferguson to Geneva: Using the Human Rights Framework to Push Forward a Vision for Racial Justice in the United States after Ferguson*, 12 HASTINGS RACE & POVERTY L.J. 121 (2015); Priscilla Ocen, *Beyond Ferguson: Integrating Critical Race Theory and the "Social Psychology of Criminal Procedure,"* in THE NEW CRIMINAL JUSTICE THINKING 226 (Sharon Dolovich & Alexandra Natapoff eds. 2017).

18 *See, e.g.*, Sustainable Economies Law Center, www.theselc.org; Gulf Coast Center for Law and Policy, www.gcclp.org/; East Bay Community Law Center, ebclc.org. *See generally* Amna Akbar, Sameer Ashar & Jocelyn Simonson, "Movement Law," unpublished manuscript presented to Law and Political Economy Summer Series, LPE Social Movements, July 22, 2020 (online) (arguing that legal academics should co-create intellectual movements with front-line organizers and lawyers, and providing examples of how these coalitions are building the new).

19 Quoted in C. Brandon Ogbunu, *How Afrofuturism Can Help the World Mend*, WIRED (July 15, 2020), www.wired.com/story/how-afrofuturism-can-help-the-world-mend.

FURTHER READINGS

1 During our first few years, after establishing a community website, we created an online "Primer" that we expanded and updated periodically by adding a new "volume" every few years. At the time of its preparation in the early 2000s, the third of the three-volume LatCrit Primer collected articles designed to provide a historical and substantive overview of the development of LatCrit theory. These early web-based versions of the Primer include chiefly the forewords and afterwords of various LatCrit symposia published to that date and written by an expanding number of international and interdisciplinary scholars.

FURTHER READINGS

Note: Although, in the interest of inclusivity and avoiding the star system, we normally strive within LatCrit to avoid featuring certain LatCrit publications over others, here we supply an abbreviated list for those instructors who wish to suggest or assign additional background on the evolution of LatCrit theory, community, and praxis. For even further study than the sources below, we recommend review of the entire history of forewords and afterwords written in connection with LatCrit symposia, with most of those sources linked at the LatCrit website, www.latcrit.com.

Steven Bender & Francisco Valdes, with Shelley Cavalieri, Jasmine Gonzalez Rose, Saru Matambanadzo, Roberto Corrada, Jorge Roig, Tayyab Mahmud, Zsea Bowmani & Anthony E. Varona, *Afterword—What's Next? Into a Third Decade of LatCrit Theory, Community, and Praxis*, 16 SEATTLE J. SOC. JUST. 823 (2018).

Steven W. Bender & Francisco Valdes, *At and Beyond Fifteen: Mapping LatCrit Theory, Community, and Praxis*, 14 HARV. LATINO L. REV. 397 (2011).

Marc-Tizoc González, Yanira Reyes, Belkys Torres & Charles R. Venator-Santiago, *The LatCrit Task Force Recommendations: Findings and Recommendations of a Self-Study of the LatCrit Board, 2009*, 18 AM. U. J. OF GENDER SOCIAL POL'Y AND L. 853 (2010).

Berta Hernandez-Truyol, Angela P. Harris & Francisco Valdes, *Afterword—Beyond the First Decade: A Forward-Looking History of LatCrit Theory, Community and Praxis*, 26 CHICANO-LATINO L. REV. 237 (2006).

Margaret E. Montoya, *LatCrit Theory: Mapping Its Intellectual and Political Foundations and Future Self-Critical Directions*, 53 U. MIAMI L. REV. 1119 (1999) (situating LatCrit politically, historically, and intellectually).

Margaret E. Montoya & Francisco Valdes, *Afterword—"Latinas/os" and Latina/o Legal Studies: A Critical and Self-Critical Review of LatCrit Theory and Legal Models of Knowledge Production*, 4 FIU L. REV. 187 (2008).

Athena D. Mutua, *Shifting Bottoms and Rotating Centers: Reflections on LatCrit III and the Black/White Paradigm*, 53 U. OF MIAMI L. REV. 1177 (1988) (discussing and assessing LatCrit techniques and methods of analysis and praxis in the context of the LatCrit III conference).

Francisco Valdes, *Coming Up: New Foundations in LatCrit Theory, Community and Praxis*, 48 CAL. W. L. REV. 505 (2012).
Francisco Valdes, *Rebellious Knowledge Production, Academic Activism, & Outsider Democracy: From Principles to Practices in LatCrit Theory, 1995 to 2008*, 8 SEATTLE J. SOC. JUST. 131 (2009).
Francisco Valdes, *Under Construction: LatCrit Consciousness, Community, and Theory*, 85 CAL. L. REV. 1087 (1997), 10 LA RAZA L.J. 1 (1998).

WEB-BASED LATCRIT PRIMER, VOLUME III, TABLE OF CONTENTS[1]

As detailed in the LatCrit Primer Volume III Table of Contents that follows, the collection there of titles of forewords and afterwords published through the LatCrit VIII conference gives an early sense of the (then) history and evolution of the LatCrit intervention.

Francisco Valdes, *Foreword, Poised at the Cusp: LatCrit Theory, Outsider Jurisprudence and Latina/o Self-Empowerment* (LatCrit I).
Elvia R. Arriola, *Foreword, March* (LatCrit II).
Elizabeth M. Iglesias & Francisco Valdes, *Afterword, Religion, Gender, Sexuality, Race and Class in Coalitional Theory: A Critical and Self-Critical Analysis of LatCrit Social Justice Agendas* (LatCrit II).
Elizabeth M. Iglesias, *Foreword, Identity, Democracy, Communicative Power, Inter/ National Labor Rights and The Evolution of LatCrit Theory and Community* (LatCrit III).
Francisco Valdes, *Afterword, Theorizing "OutCrit" Theories: Coalitional Method and Comparative Jurisprudential Experience—RaceCrits, QueerCrits and LatCrits* (LatCrit III).
Kevin R. Johnson, *Foreword, Celebrating LatCrit Theory: What Do We Do When the Music Stops?* (LatCrit IV).
Mary Romero, *Afterword, Historicizing and Symbolizing a Racial Ethnic Identity: Lessons for Coalition Building with a Social Justice Agenda* (LatCrit IV).
Margaret E. Montoya, *Foreword, Class in LatCrit: Theory and Praxis in a World of Economic Inequality* (LatCrit V).
Guadalupe T. Luna, *Foreword, America Latina and Jurisprudential Associations* (LatCrit VI).
Ediberto Román, *Afterword, LatCrit VI: Outsider Jurisprudence and Looking Beyond Imagined Borders* (LatCrit VI).
Roque Martín Saavedra, *Miradas Desde El Sur: Introducción al Simposio Latcrit Sobre Derecho Internacional Y Derecho Comparado, Buenos Aires, Agosto de 2003*.
Francisco Valdes, *Foreword, City and Citizen: Community-Making As Legal Theory and Social Struggle* (LatCrit VIII).
Kevin Johnson, *Foreword, LatCrit Goes International* (ICC).

INDEX

ABOUT THE AUTHORS

STEVEN W. BENDER is Professor of Law at Seattle University School of Law. He writes in diverse areas of law, politics, history, and culture, and his fourteen published books include *Greasers and Gringos: Latinos, Law, and the American Imagination* (New York University Press 2003), *Tierra y Libertad: Land, Liberty, and Latino Housing* (New York University Press 2010), *Run for the Border: Vice and Virtue in U.S.-Mexico Border Crossings* (New York University Press 2012), and *Mea Culpa: Lessons on Law and Regret from U.S. History* (New York University Press 2015).

FRANCISCO VALDES is Professor of Law at the University of Miami, earned a B.A. in 1978 from the University of California at Berkeley, a JD with honors in 1984 from the University of Florida College of Law, and a JSM in 1991 and a JSD in 1994 from Stanford Law School. He publishes extensively, speaks regularly at academic conferences and similar events, and teaches in the areas of U.S. constitutional law, systemic advocacy, and critical theory.